AMY LOWELL

WITHDRAWN

AMY LOWELL

Clement Wood

NEW YORK
HAROLD VINAL
1926

PS
3523
O88
28

PRINTED IN THE UNITED STATES OF AMERICA BY
THE VAIL-BALLOU PRESS, BINGHAMTON, N. Y.

To
the memory of
JOHN KEATS

CONTENTS

AMY LOWELL

THE BREACH IN THE WALL

I

American poetry is a young and rising shore, measured beside the intricate continental expanse, the reach of ancient broken hillland, of English song. The English folk ballads had lifted the soil like woodland violets, stern Langland and gay Chaucer had sung in the morning, before the prow of the *Santa Maria* grounded on the Caribbean beach, and new-found America became an out-put of old Europe. The wide, high music of Elizabeth's day, the winding glamour of Spenser, the heaving wonder of Shakespeare and the dramatists, the heaven-song of Campion and the lutanists—all this had dulled, before Jamestown and Plymouth Rock felt the lasting tread of English comers. Puritan Milton and the cavalier minnesingers, and then the long age of the rhymed epigram, sparkled and dimmed, before Concord, Valley Forge and Yorktown had been written in as slogans in the glossary of man's slow stumble toward liberty. A new burst of lyric beauty made the mother air sweet, Burns and Blake, Wordsworth and Coleridge, Scott and Byron, Shelley and Keats—and still America, young and tongue-tied, stared toward the home-land crests.

Not that we were entirely dumb: there had been juvenile Colonial stammerings of fugitive Southern lyricists, of Bay Psalm Books, of such provincial Shakespeares as the Reverend Michael Wigglesworth, whose "laborious rhymes" made him a gem among Harvard graduates. Silenced vocally in his pastorate by an affection of the lungs, Wigglesworth lifted strains which passed through six American and one London edition.

> Still was the night, serene and bright,
>   When all men sleeping lay;
> Calm was the season, and carnal reason
>   Thought so 'twould last for aye.

Thus cantered his *The Day of Doom, or a Poetical Description of the Great and Last Judgment, with a Short Discourse about Eternity*, its Puritan rigor mollified a bit, as when he allots to the infants subject to damnation,——

2

AMY LOWELL

> Although in bliss
> They may not hope to dwell,
> Still unto them He will allow
> The easiest room in hell.

Somewhat in this mood America began its song. England, with voices that sang at heaven's gate, saw no reason to tremble for the repose of its poetic crown.

Bryant was born the year before Keats; but the New York and New England groups stretched principally through Victoria's reign. The other side heard Browning, Tennyson, Swinburne, and their compeers; only in Poe and Whitman, upon this shore, did we hear poetry to be mentioned quietly beside England's best. When the first American age of poetry passed, a fallow half century swung in, hardly broken by the brief troubled music of Sidney Lanier, and the beauty of Emily Dickinson's walled singing. Today, England drowses through the pipings of the tepid Georgians, for all of the young poignancy of Housman, the thunder of Chesterton, the surge of Masefield, the small gray magic of de la Mare. And America today —is she still a laggard in poetry, that concentrated essence of the soul's uttered desires?

3

Shortly after 1910, an epidemic of poetry swept through these States. It was as contagious as laughter or the measles, and almost as virulent as the *virus Elizabethiensis*. It rooted in Whitman, at times diluted through a Gallic sieve, and Poe; in drained New England and the adolescent West; in the Congo and Spoon River; in the city called Han and the ticking of Eternity. America rioted in poetry. If it did not usurp the headlines, it at least reached the stage where a man who confessed to poetry was not at once committed for observation. Soon after 1915, the vast pot had simmered down somewhat, and above the ebullient cacophony there stood out as the dominant figures of the poetic renascence in the public eye, Edgar Lee Masters, Amy Lowell, Robert Frost, Edwin Arlington Robinson, Carl Sandburg, and Vachel Lindsay. The critical eye, in the main, was similar in its appraisal. Ten years dragged by, with Europe red with war and its aftermath, and America tardily torn by the same slow social suicide. In the public eye, American poetry was still the same six, with the possible addition of Edna St. Vincent Millay and Elinor Wylie; though critical opinion cast eyes askance at the later

4

work of Masters and Lindsay, though a rare Hosea cried out against the bard of Brookline, though a more frequent dilettante of the intelligentsia squealed a wild pæan to strange sayers like Eliot, Kreymborg, Bodenheim.

And then, without warning, the great besieger bore up against the citadel in the night, and tore a breach that let in a hateful void of sky. Amy Lowell, vigorous fighter, brilliant innovator and artificer of words, had died—died in her fifty-first year, when the popular home acclaim to her two volume *John Keats* had just raised it to the best seller class, and when harsh overseas words had just begun to come in. It was Death's first blow at the important figures in the modern revival of our poetry; and it is not an exaggeration to say that the victim was, in the eyes of no inconsiderable portion of our land, preeminently modern American poetry itself. Her glittering verses, her militant prefaces and critical studies, her constant packed platform appearances had elevated her to a commanding place. She died—America drew a sudden startled breath.

Amy Lowell, in her verse and her ample theories about verse, was, is, and may be an important formative influence upon the poets of today and tomorrow. Her words speak for themselves, at least on the surface. Had they best be left so, with perhaps an orderly eulogy in the nature of a biography, and a few academic volumes of undiscriminating tribute? A Rotary eulogy, with sloganeer boosts. . . . Or is this the hour for the critic to speak: that what was enduring and well-visioned in her work may be seen as such, and may influence as such; and that what was momentary only and woven of shoddy shall be so ticketed, lest, as too often, the men and women lashed into poetry by the inescapable inner compulsion, "consecrate the flicker, not the flame"? It is a wise emendation, *de mortuis nil nisi veritatem,* "of the dead speak nothing but the truth"—the truth, as well as it may be seen. A temporary harm, which breeds a permanent warping of values, may come from uncritical adulation, in the dawn after death no less than at any other time. Now, while her echoes ring in our ears, and her still unspread words are damp on the printed page, is the time for at least a tentative appraisal of what she stood for, and what she achieved.

There is need for walking delicately in the

presence of such a task. In dealing with a contemporary, the air above the living head or the wilting flowers is sullen with prejudices and drizzly with unearned reverences, in perhaps every instance. One is on bedrock in venturing a pronouncement upon the worth of the unearthed Sapphic fragments, even if it be a bedrock largely of ignorance; one has neither been honored nor slighted at board by the singer of Lesbos, nor suffered from her loose praise or blame; the faint high song has neither a cloud of waspish detractors nor a fanatic claque. There is an inevitable illusion of the near; yet intelligence may discount this, and see the living fern as no more and no less than the darker lacework stoned toward immortality in the coal measures. The poet cannot evade the responsibility for true talk on his own living craft. We have Symons' astute word for it that only in the hands of a poet can criticism of poetry be the winged thing it should be. The poet, says Baudelaire, must contain a critic; and his criticism must emanate from the same deeps of his spirit, sharpened by the same whittle of the intellect, that in its time produces his own poetry.

7

Criticism, Symons elaborates, is a valuation of forces, and is indifferent to their direction. Its aim is to distinguish what is essential in the work of a writer. To do this it must interpret, share publicly the poet's aim, let his ware be sampled. It concerns itself with the root principles of human nature, with fundamental ideas. It must innately reveal the deepest philosophy of the critic throughout, if it is to be more than verbal back-scratching, friendly or the reverse. Paul Elmer More said well that it must stand entirely aloof from the currents of the hour, judging men and things from the larger circles of time; it must be emancipated, as far as is humanly possible, from the illusions of the present. For critical acceptance is one of the gateways every candidate must pass toward accepted greatness: and perdurable greatness means inclusion among the few whom the straining dust-filled eyes of man keep ever in view.

Again, in this valuation of esthetic forces, the critic must realize that, other achievements being equal, the experimenter in art is a more vivid force than the traditionalist. Art among men regresses constantly into the crustacean; the decried innovation becomes the dogma crypted in its chitinous shell,—becomes a Medusa's poll, turning to bloodless stone those who gaze admiringly upon it. The traditionalist finds his tools, his materials, at hand; the experimenter alters old tools, creates new ones, lets down his net into the undersea of human sensations and conceptions, and draws up strange new prizes to broaden the matter of poetry. The traditionalist cuts the groove deeper—and the groove must be deep for the car to run steadily; the experimenter lifts the dull glass, poetry, to reflect constantly widening panoramas of life. Poetry at best lags far behind the life it mirrors. The experimenter aids in bringing poetry continually back toward life. And, without life, poetry dies, remaining no more than the eviscerated barnacle shell upon the moving hull.

Other achievements being equal, we said. And—if they are not? There comes in the need for further differentiation. Moreover, the technique of an art, for instance, poetry, grows somewhat as life evolves; that is, with a multiplicity of experimentations, only a few of which are of permanent benefit. Lester Ward's dictum upon the evolution of life:

With the life force pushing in all conceivable directions, as from the center toward every point on the surface of a sphere, every possible process must have been tried.

This applies no less to poetry than to organic development. Strange living eccentricities and sports have come and come repeatedly, sterile for their very eccentricity: and poetry knows these too. Experimentations, then, must be weighed honestly, without prejudice, as to their aim and achievement: and if the result is seen to be eccentricity beyond ameliorative aid, if it is a jerry-built verbal insanity or a songless, senseless prose or spindrift of disintegrated ideas and phrases abandoned by a receding swirl of mindless fury, it must be so labelled.

Knowledge, then, and detachment, and a certain judicial quality, all must be present. But these are not enough. No literary criticism henceforth will reach its full worth, which is unaware of what modern science has contributed to an understanding of the artist and his product. More than two decades ago, Freud, followed by Jung, Adler and others, gave mankind the beginning of an approach to critical understanding, of inestimable value as a supplement to older esthetic modes of appraisal. An art product, an epic, a sonnet, from this viewpoint, expresses, superficially or latently, some desire of the artist, phrased as desire or as a thing accomplished: poems are, to use the technical term, wish-fulfillments. Moreover, approval or acceptance of a poem is deeply tinged with an identification of the poet's wish-fulfillment with our own. The poet, whether he be Shakespeare or James Byron Elmore of Alamo, Indiana, pictures himself and his reach, upward or downward, in his poetry: the poet is his poetry, when the product is rightly seen. The picture revealed by the poem may be scanty enough: but it is more accurate than the most approved camera biography can give. This critical method lifts *Endymion* from a meaningless jumble or a catch-all of misty abstractions, to what it was to Keats himself: a reiterated spiritual autobiography of his life down to the time of its writing. The poem is neither an awkward phrasing of "the soul's thirst for Beauty" (Colvin) nor an expansion of the "basic theory that love is the principal of all things and 'creative of essential Beauty' " (Amy Lowell) ; it is the wish-fulfilled heaven of "Mister

11

John Keats five feet high," who had been rejected by such earthly women as he had yet
desired, and who built his inverted dream-
world in which Adonis yielded to Venus,
Arethusa to Alpheus, and Glaucus to Circe; a
dream-world in which the great mythic creations of selective and rejecting chastity yielded
to love; a dream-world in which the heavens
gave to John Keats what the earth had refused
him. This critical method does as much for
other poetry. That poem is greatest, to you,
which best phrases your own desires, either as
a lyric cry or symbolized as a wish achieved in
story or drama. Greatness may be redefined,
from this viewpoint, as the quality inhering in
a work which phrases, to the largest group of
people over the longest stretch of time, their
own deepest longings. The old definitions of
greatness referred to acceptance merely; this
new one indicates the reason for the acceptance.

Accordingly, a poet's work must be studied
in the light of the new psychology, with the
certainty that two chief results will follow. We
will secure from the poetry a portrait of the
author: of the elements of his or her life that
seemed significant to the poet, and were repeated

for the pleasure of the repetition, or as symbols of things yet unachieved; of the conflicts, un-fulfillments, and decisions that complete the likeness of the poet's spirit. Biography—the interpretation of a life—is a dismembered torso, or less, when it deals only with things done: things desired that were left undone are at times the more tremendous in revelation and influence; the avoided alternatives may be the key to the real life. More than this, this method of baring the poet's longing will reveal whether that longing is unique and non-general, or whether it words a common cry of many hearts. If the latter, granting that the technique suffices, we have an approach toward greatness; if the problems embodied in the poetry are limited to one individual, or to a class numerically insignificant, the poet may be a laureate of that individual or class, but cannot be more. Such a method must give coherence to the study; and must render it the reverse of dull. For dullness means life-lessness; and a living study of poetry cannot be dull. The careful marshalling of details must, in flashes of revelation, word itself in general-izations which may assume the quality of epigrams; these are in essence akin to poetry's concentration of reaches toward the truth. In the hands of an inept citic, such a method will give results that sag inexpressibly; in the hands of a qualified critic, it will give the truest illumination of which man is yet capable.

Criticism is something more than a mere digression from the poet's function of expression. It is an interpretation of the critic as well as the criticized, and is more than this: it is creative in a high degree. For poets cannot avoid being social beings, specialized into expression. No poet stands alone, uninfluenced by the poetic past and the poetic present; in such cases, the danger of merely repeating blunders long phrased and cured is almost inevitable. The poets of an age, I have long held, are more than individuals: they are spokesmen for the age, knit toward oneness by this rôle; they are, in a deep sense, one body, one tongue, disjointedly seeking to voice the age's word. The future will grant to this age, as to any age, only a limited sprinkling of pages in the amplest anthologies of man's concentrated speech. The task of the living poets is not primarily to preempt space for themselves, but to make the age's pages as ample, as worthy, as enduring, as flawless technically, as possible. A

14

poet has done much less than his task who refuses the hand of help to another poet: both gain when the halting phrase of the second is lifted, by the fragmentary insight of the first, into a word demanding long memory. What I have achieved has been due, more largely than outsiders dream, to the aid of others: the hour will not come when I will withhold my aid from any of my fellows in this strangely unified body and tongue of today's poets. Miss Lowell was outstanding in her aid to others, in the direction that she held worthy.

Criticism, then, is creative, in that it indicates to the criticized and to the hosts of singers here and to come what is worthy, and what is not: and, when the criticized has passed beyond the push of living words, the critical product is still a shaper of poems to be, a midwife, or better, a co-begetter, of today's word and tomorrow's. Most of all, this responsibility calls upon the critic for all of the sincerity, all of the clarity of vision and utterance, all of the naked courage of soul, that he has in him to give.

With these things in mind, let us turn to the bright career of Amy Lowell, and see what, as person and utterance, she had to contribute, and contributed, to our living stream of song.

II

The American Lowells trace back to Perceval Lowle or Lowell, who emigrated from Somersetshire to Massachusetts Bay in 1639, and was the founder of the family in the colonies. The family included a member of the Continental Congress, John Lowell, a distinguished libertarian, whose "All men are born free and equal," in the Massachusetts State Constitution, was construed by the State Supreme Court to abolish slavery. One of John Lowell's sons, Charles Lowell, was father of James Russell Lowell, poet, critic, editor, and diplomat. Another son, Francis Cabot Lowell, founded cotton manufacture in the United States; from him the city of Lowell, Massachusetts, was named. John Lowell, an older son of the earlier John, was a forthright opponent of Mr. Jefferson's democratic policies, and a distinguished figure in agriculture, earning for himself the title of "The

16

Columella of New England." He was the ancestor of three generations who were successively heads of the Lowell Institute of Boston, which furnishes free public lectures. The last of these, Abbott Lawrence Lowell, is now president of Harvard University; a brother, Percival Lowell, was a well-known astronomer, best remembered for his insistence that the "canals" of Mars indicate life and civilization on that planet. Amy Lowell, born in Brookline, Massachusetts, on February 9, 1874, was a sister of these two.

Jean Catel, an appreciator of the poet, writes of her:

"I am Amy Lowell, of Brookline, Massachusetts," she used to say when she was a little girl. She remained that little girl. She kept her pride of her vaguely felt tradition.

She received her education in private schools. Beyond this slim fact, the published records are largely silent as to her childhood and life for the first thirty-eight years. Her intimate friends have told me, she herself told me that, during these years, she studied intently. Later we shall take up that aspect of her life. There are fragmentary records of her childhood in her own volumes; this was inescapable. In her first book, *A Dome of Many-Coloured Glass,* published in 1912, when the poet had reached thirty-eight, we have, in *A Fairy Tale,*

> On winter nights beside the nursery fire
> We read the fairy tale, while glowing coals
> Builded its pictures—

an idyllic opening, pointing to a sheltered beginning for the little girl.   The poem alters to a mature bitterness:

Always shall I be teased with semblances,
With cruel impostures, which I trust awhile,
Then dash to pieces, as a careless boy
Flings a kaleidoscope, which shattering
Strews all the ground about with careless sherds.

In the section, *Verses for Children,* we have more material.   She asks the sea-shell to sing her

> A song of ships, and sailor men,
>   And parrots, and tropical trees,
> Of islands lost in the Spanish Main
> Which no man ever may find again.

Fairy stories, adventure stories, and then a poem to fringed gentians beside a lake:

> It's just a lake of lovely flowers,
> And my Mamma says they are ours;
> But they are not like those we grow
> To be our very own, you know.

18

The garden flowers may be picked; but not the wild gentians—for they would die of home-sickness before night. *The Painted Ceiling* adds to the picture:

My Grandpapa lives in a wonderful house,
　　With a great many windows and doors,
There are stairs that go up, and stairs that go
　　　　down,
　　And such beautiful, slippery floors.

But of all of the rooms, even mother's and mine,
　　And the book-room, and parlour and all,
I like the green dining-room so much the best
　　Because of its ceiling and wall.

Overhead is fruit—apples, pears, grapes and more:

They tumble and tumble, but never come down
　　Though I've stood underneath a long while
With my mouth open wide, for I always have
　　　　hoped
　　Just a cherry would drop from the pile.

She seeks to reach them:

I've given up hope, and I feel I shall die
　　Without having accomplished the deed,

just because she is short, she says. Yet the poet was thirty-eight when this volume reached publication; and "without having accomplished the deed" may have grown to some more mature meaning in her mind. Too much weight need not be given to this: but again and again some verse, apparently trivial, phrases the main trend of the poet's cry. This may be laid aside, unless ample corroboration obtrudes itself. *The Crescent Moon* is lightly sung, with roses gathered in the milky way—

> All to carry home to mother.
> Oh! what will she say!
>
> Little rocking, sailing moon,
>   Do you hear me shout—Ahoy!
> Just a little nearer, moon,
>   To please a little boy.

Here is the mother, twice before referred to; and the child is pictured as "a little boy." *The Fairy Tale* referred to "a careless boy"; the sea shell song refers to adventure stories, more usual as boyish fare than girl's readings. *Climbing* is a bright picture of apple-tree sport; there is a tribute to the "naughty little speckled trout" and to the wind—

He twirls my kite till it breaks its string,

AMY LOWELL

and one reference to "The flag in front of the school unfurls," which faintly shadows some school she attended. Of the Pleiades she says,

> I've known them all my life, you see.

She says of the little angel boy, whose toys they are,

> I wish he'd come down and play with me.
> We'd have such fun, for it would be
> A most unusual thing for boys
> To feel that they had stars for toys!

A boy's kaleidoscope, adventure stories, a kite —and the poet as little boy, whenever she is pictured as boy or girl—with no mention thus far of dolls or girls' games—strange that, from the start, the poet pictures herself as a little boy!

In the third book, we have *A Roxbury Garden,* telling how Minna and Stella play at hoops, at battledore and shuttlecock, and garden games. In *Penumbra,* in *Pictures of the Floating World,* we get this definite childhood picture:

> The old house will still be here,
> The old house which has known me since the beginning.
> The walls which have watched me while I played:

21

Soldiers, marbles, paper-dolls,
Which have protected me and my books.

The front-door will gaze down among the old
    trees
Where, as a child, I hunted ghosts and Indians;
It will look out on the wide gravel sweep
Where I rolled my hoop,
And at the rhododendron bushes
Where I caught black-spotted butterflies.

This sincere memory note ties together what
we have already reached, and points to an autobiographical background for all the verses
quoted. As a child, Amy Lowell played boys'
games as much or more than girls' games; and
from the start, she speaks as if she regarded herself as a boy in childhood.

One element is missing—and its omission is
significant. Her appearance bodily has been
emphasized in all intimate accounts of her; we
will soon come to these. Her body was plump
rather than graceful, and her appearance and
conduct tended toward the masculine. It was
unavoidable, in such a case, that other children
were less considerate of the Lowell name and
fame than adults would be, and there must have
been sick moments when she was the butt of

some childish ridicule, no matter how well-bred. This came at first as a horrid shock: and soon enough a person of Amy Lowell's abounding vigor must build up a defensive shell, to hide her inner irk. So well did she retreat behind her masculine defenses, that she found out that the thing worked admirably. This gave her a sense of power: she had created an answer to the taunts. The sense of power, and the longing for more of the sweet taste of domineeringness, made her turn her defensive mechanism outward: the crust became a weapon of offense. Again it worked admirably: she was "Amy Lowell of Brookline, Massachusetts." She grew early to an enjoyment of this domineering trait; and, in return for the inward hurt that she felt was unearned, she reciprocated by hurting others: by a growth towards sadism, or a delight in inflicting pain. If this analysis is accurate, we may expect to find definite sadism cropping up in her poetry. The omission, of this growth from a girl untouched by the outward environment to the girl protected by her defensive crust and able to use it outwardly to inflict pain on others, is significant: it points to inner pain that she could not share with her readers.

There is little more to learn of the first thirty-eight years of her life, except in the long poem to *The Boston Athenæum*:

Thou dear and well-loved haunt of happy hours,
How often in some distant gallery,
Gained by a little painful spiral stair,
Far from the halls and corridors where throng
The crowd of casual readers, have I passed
Long, peaceful hours seated on the floor
Of some retired nook, all lined with books.

She adjudges,

For books are more than books, they are the life,
The very heart and core of ages past,
The reason why men lived, and worked, and died,
The essence and quintessence of their lives.

This must phrase her reach toward truth, of course, rather than absolute truth. It was Walt Whitman who wrote,

Poems distill'd from poems pass away.

Her apostrophe continues,

We know ourselves the richer to have sat
Upon this dusty floor and dreamed our
    dreams. . . .
For this is ours! Every twist and turn
Of every narrow stair is known and loved;

24

Each nook and cranny is our very own;
The dear, old sleepy place is full of spells
For us, by right of long inheritance. . . .
And here that veiled, but ever smouldering fire
Of race, which rarely seen yet never dies,
Springs up afresh and warms us with its heat.

Here we have her, then, for some portion of the preparative period, climbing the "little painful spiral stair," sitting on the floor, getting "life" from the books, re-warmed by the "smouldering fire of race," her pride in her ancestry.

The first published poem recorded in Poole's *Index of Periodical Literature* is *Fixed Idea,* appearing in *The Atlantic Monthly* for August, 1910, and reappearing in her first volume. The next year saw two more periodical poems; and then, in 1912, at the age of thirty-eight, she published *A Dome of Many-Coloured Glass,* entitled from Shelley's *Adonais.* Its poetic worth we will consider later. It was well received by the run of newspaper critics: the *Buffalo Express* found a "pure lyrical quality"; the home *Boston Evening Transcript* grudged "these poems arouse interest, and justify it by the result"; the home *Boston Sunday Globe* found the verses "based on some of the loftiest ideals"; the *Pittsburg Index*

25

called them "vari-coloured jewels, some people will think."

The modern poetic renascence had hardly lifted its head; yet Sara Teasdale, William Rose Benet, Vachel Lindsay and Edwin Arlington Robinson were producing memorable work, and having it acclaimed; Edna St. Vincent Millay's *Renascence* appeared during the year in *The Lyric Year;* Harriet Monroe's *Poetry* and William Stanley Braithwaite's annual summaries had commenced.

Critical opinion consisted of two opposing camps: the classical authorities and the touters for the American awakening. By both, Miss Lowell's volume was largely neglected. Yet her inner compulsion must have been powerfully insistent upon receiving resounding public acclaim. How could she wrest applause from an audience largely unaware of her existence?

We have come, I think, to the great turning-point of her life. There are two gateways to immediate applause, if we omit the unpretentious lowbrow laureateship bestowed by witless shouts upon Walt Mason, Eddie Guest, Robert W. Service, and their peers, and the ephemeral lauds for the over-erotic. One is by slow solid

achievement: a tardy process, at times pointed toward a posthumous goal; the other, by artistic eccentricity. Those without the patience to wait for the former hurl themselves into the latter, if they feel the painful itch to acquire a special-delivery reputation. Her trips to England, occurring about this time, brought Amy Lowell in contact with the London experimentalists headed by Ezra Pound, a group who called themselves "Des Imagistes" or The Imagists. She joined the group, became its outstanding leader, and thus made her decision. Let me quote Jean Catel again for a glimpse at her attitude during this time:

She bore the Victorians, her older neighbors, and the rising generation of poets, her younger neighbors, the same grudge. They both stood in her way to conquest. Children will be masters.

He does not apply this specifically to the period in question, but to her general attitude. That attitude was rooted in her childhood. The tepid reception of her first book made it virulent. We are of necessity walking gingerly on ground somewhat conjectural; yet it must have been in such a frame of mind—of bafflement at non-acceptance, and fierce insistence upon achieving acceptance somehow, and soon, that she espoused the Imagist cause.

During the winter of 1913, Ezra Pound (perhaps aided by Miss Lowell) collected a number of poems illustrating the Imagist point of view, which were printed together in a little volume, *Des Imagistes*, in April, 1914, over a New York imprint. Richard Aldington is represented, among others, by his young borrow of a passing fragment of Shakespeare's, where Antony says to Cleopatra—

> I found you as a morsel cold upon
> Dead Cæsar's trencher,

which Aldington uses as the climax to his *Lesbia* in this fashion:

> You morsel left half cold on Cæsar's plate.

out of a thicket of anemic tributes to minor classical deities. We have also H. D. (Hilda Doolittle), F. S. Flint, Skipwith Cannell, William Carlos Williams, James Joyce, Ford Madox Hueffer, Allen Upward, John Cournos, Pound himself, and Miss Lowell's *In a Garden*, a love poem containing:

28

And I wished for night and you. . . .
Night and the water, and you in your whiteness,
   bathing!

Louis Untermeyer describes the reception to this
volume:

It does not seem possible that this set of honest
and almost platitudinous principles (the Imagist
credo) could have evoked the storm of argument, fury and downright vilification that broke
after the indomitable Miss Lowell began to
champion them.

Grant that this is overdrawn, yet there are
embers of truth in it. In any case, Pound soon
went over to the Vorticists, Hueffer returned to
his prose, Cournos to his art criticism, while Williams and Cannell joined the further left wing
christened "Others." Miss Lowell added to the
remnant of Aldington, H. D., Flint, and herself,
two more—D. H. Lawrence and John Gould
Fletcher—and saw to the publication of three
annual Imagist anthologies, the first appearing
in 1915. Meanwhile, the year before witnessed
Miss Lowell's second volume, *Sword Blades and
Poppy Seed*, with the first of her militant prefaces. The altering attitudes of Boston may be
gathered from an informative *Memory Sketch*

for a Biographer by Elizabeth Shepley Sergeant
in *The New Republic:*

When, straining against Bostonian precedent, she
not only made friends with actresses, and gave
plays on Sunday afternoons, but actually published "free" verse in *The Atlantic Monthly,* her
career and aims were taken as a sort of eccentric
scandal. It was not until her poetic leadership
was acclaimed from continent to continent that
she became a jewel in the crown of a great
Massachusetts family.

We have not yet pictured the bodily poet:
and this is as good a time as any to do so. I met
her first in 1917, and two or three times thereafter: she did not materially alter in appearance
during the years that followed. I came to the
interview with a mind full of legends of her
stoutness, her big black cigars, her dictatorial
belligerency. My first impression was different
from all of these: it was of an abiding charm of
personality, a spiritual magnetism, that disposed
me to confiding friendship from the start. I
have met only two other people who radiated
such an overflowing attractiveness: Theodore
Roosevelt, and John F. Tucker, the latter the
grotesque little man who was for years secretary
of the Twilight Club in New York City. The

legendary Miss Lowell was as real as the magnetism; but the latter should be emphasized first, in
describing her. Her bodily frame was exces-
sively stout and ungainly; her face held something childish, self-consciously prim, and almost
mediocre, with a sleek urbanity of self-assurance
grown from her long cultural background. She
uttered cordial allegiance to poetry, and told me
that after all, my function was not that of a
voice of protest, but that of a "serf to beauty."
My XIXth *Eagle Sonnet*, in *The Tide Comes In*,
was seeded in the talk with her; the opening half
line was first written with the phrase she used.
When we came to the matter upon which she
had summoned me, her aggrievement at my
judgment that her *Tendencies in Modern American Poetry* was a volume of sublimated log-
rolling, she became impassioned in protestations
of her disinterestedness. When I explained
more amply how fully the book bore out my
contention, she broke down and cried—not so
much outraged at my attitude, for we remained
and parted as friends, but as if baffled and impotent at her inability to convert me, by her
presence, to her belief in the book's impartiality.
I was honored with the gift of one of her cigars,

and found it too strong to finish. Later talks
with her added little to this first encounter.

The New Statesman described her:

She was of immense physique, with a massive
head, a brow that suggested a vast reservoir of
brain force, a voice that told of arrogant and
conquering vitality. . . . She was masculine,
overwhelming. . . . A good round oath was as
natural to her lips as the uncompromising cigar
that gave flavor to her after-dinner talk and
kept her going through nights of literary labor,
for she habitually worked till dawn.

Miss Sergeant's article in *The New Republic*,
already referred to, holds a fine full length portrait of the poet. In addition to a "passionate
and untrammelled heart," Miss Lowell had had
to suffer—

physical illness, disability, and a kind of fleshly
discomfort that no woman could bear in youth
without suffering self-consciousness, and the
sense of a lost Paradise.

Her figure, which her own eyes "could not
admire," was regularly "encased in a trim uni-
form of rich dark satin, with stiff boned col-
lar." Her mansion of Sevenels, "high, square,
mansard-roofed, brown stone," in the more

staid gardened section of Brookline, was an outward symbol of much abiding stability indoors. Here she was born, and lived, and died; here, and in her poetry. Not in the formal lower part of the house, but high under the slated eaves, was her workroom and actual dwelling:

Her wide low bed was the very nucleus of this central cell; it had exactly sixteen pillows. . . . I have seen her reading in that bed under a black umbrella in the bright light of midafternoon, smoking, of course, the equally black cigars.

Despite her vast tiled bathroom, "Amy Lowell en deshabille was a New England vestal." In action, Miss Sergeant pictures her as a New England autocrat of the old school, foreordained to preempting the foremost place:

She could not help arousing sensation wherever she went—love or hate, curiosity, suspense, drama. She lived dramatically, and opulently, always for spectators.

When she reached her accustomed suite at the Belmont Hotel, in New York City, where she stopped several times a year, every large mirror had to be swathed in black, every clock stopped, and the sixteen pillows produced. Every clock

33

stopped. . . . Her two most profound influences were Eleanora Duse and Ada Russell, the latter the devoted friend who lived during the last years with Miss Lowell at Sevenels, and who is her literary executrix. Both of these women were actresses. The poet had an advertising flair, a publicity sense, almost unequalled. It was she more than anyone else who put the "new poetry" "on the map," states Miss Sergeant; and there is little to quarrel with here.

As to her habits of work,

She began to write when others retire to rest, went to bed as early birds arise, sleeping the morning away, breakfasting at two or three in the afternoon, delving with her secretaries till dark, . . . slowly dressing for a formal dinner, and beginning the day's work again at eleven or midnight.

There may be nothing significant in the fact that her life chronologically was perverse, from the standpoint of the normal man or woman. To each his or her own routine: though most prefer the day for work, and the night for relaxation and sleep.

Miss Lowell, the article continues, was bountiful in giving; but she made it a point of pride

34

"never to loan a book from her fine library."

One of the most distinguished critics in America, born before the Civil War, a poet and college professor of the highest standing, received permission to call at Sevenels to examine Miss Lowell's first edition of Keats's poems. He told, humbly and a bit puzzled, what happened: "She let me see the book; she opened it, and let me see the pages; she would not let me hold it in my hands."

She was as autocratic in dealing with friends, servants, dependents.

It was unthinkable that their lives should revolve in individual orbits, that they should choose their own doctors, take their own vacations, live in cities where she was not. Her real predilection, she declared, was for a society of slaves.

We begin to see the immense egotism that heaved behind the massive face—a baffled egotism that determined to wring from an unwilling world such tribute as an empress might envy. When she reached New York City, she did not visit editors and publishers; she notified them to call upon her. On their arrival, she announced to them which poems they would be permitted to publish. There was no question of accepting or rejecting her work—she laid down the law. Her right was rooted only in her preemption of it. An infrequent editor refused to be so bull-dozed; whereupon she became graciously merely a writer, anxious for his editorial approval. Her seven Scotch sheep dogs were pampered like crown princes, until she decided she would keep them no further; then, instead of finding other homes for them, or selling them, she had them killed. Dogs, at least, must be a society of slaves. Miss Sergeant refers to "that forthright, buccaneering maleness of her."

This quality impressed all who saw her. The friend continues:

Amy Lowell scarcely belonged even in her own garden, among poppies and blue salvia.

Hers was primarily an indoor existence, and she realized, as midnight approached, that all the external paraphernalia,

the ice water and pillows and black cigars, the great house and American name cannot make a poet. They can help construct a celebrity.

Here we must pause a second, to wonder if we have reached bedrock. She was, at least, undeniably a celebrity. Of her poetry and its creation, Miss Lowell herself wrote:

The poem will not be denied, to refuse to write it would be a greater torture. It tears its way out of the brain, splintering and breaking its passage—and yet to have no poem to write is the worst state of all. Truly a poet's life is not a happy one. Broken and shattered when creating, urged always to a strain which cannot heal save through immense pain, peaceful only in the occasional consciousness of a tolerable achievement—certainly the poor creature must be born to his calling, for no man would take on such an existence willingly.

This is undoubtedly over-protestation; yet it is significant. One important thing about Amy Lowell is that she, throughout her career, clearly visualized her achievement, and its limitations. She was not modest about her work—there is little dissent on that. There is a courteous mock modesty that could let Shakespeare write of his sonnets "this poor rhyme." This might even have been a mood of strange abasement. But soon enough he was saying,

And thou in this shalt find thy monument,
When tyrants' crests and tombs of brass are
    spent. . . .

37

Your name from hence immortal life shall
have. . . .

Not marble, nor the gilded monuments
Of princes, shall outlive this powerful rhyme.

Throughout this study, we shall arrive at no
judgment upon Miss Lowell's work harsher than
her own vision of it, and her own wording of it.
In the quotation above, she wrote of herself:

peaceful only in the occasional consciousness of
a tolerable achievement.

Tolerable poetry is like a tolerably fresh egg.
Perhaps elsewhere she will change her attitude;
for this present, let this be noted and remembered.

The Sergeant portrait says that Miss Lowell
"could at least die for poetry," in connection
with the Keats biography, by

allowing her working nights to impinge more
and more seriously on her sleeping days over a
period of years.

With clear vision the friend describes her as of
the great New England tradition, the essentially
bookish tradition derived more from letters than
from life.

38

AMY LOWELL

Jean Catel seeks to picture more the soul of Amy Lowell:

A diluted personality, a childlike fancy for all passing shadows and ephemeral hues of the sky, a difficult imagination—she gave us that, when we needed and looked for a precise vision from the new world.

With Gallic penetration he says that her work has not the resonance of the cosmos. The hues and the perfumes that throng its pages convey little or nothing of the real perfume and hues of the air.

His dictum is that she used (and abused) the symbols that were the poetic stock of Wilde, Baudelaire, Mallarme, Yeats, and others; that she is already reduced to the level of the Victorians. The reason for this he finds in that "she knew life only through symbols of symbols":

A park screened her windows from the street, and in the park were lovely trees and rare flowers. She led an enchanted life. She was the sleeping beauty of the castle.

Miss Lowell, in the most revealing poem in her first book, used the same symbol for herself. For all that, Catel insists that she was a poet, because her expression, whatever it was, was rhythmical. And nobody will deny that rhythm is one element of poetry. Only, Amy Lowell mistook rhythm for the essence of it and worked accordingly.

This is as lacking in penetration as a dead jellyfish. No intelligent person will deny that rhythm is also one element of prose. There is rhythm, excellent accurate metrical rhythm, in most poor newspaper verse. M. Catel has raised a question; for the present, we must let it rest, as we continue to detail her achievements during these years.

Sword Blades and Poppy Seeds, with its bellicose preface, appeared in 1914: the spokesmen for the "new poetry," as well as the old, capitulated with hardly an exception. Josephine Preston Peabody, Harriet Monroe, united with Richard Le Gallienne and Arthur Davison Ficke to praise the book. To poetry, she says, she has always bound herself:

"My life? And is that all you crave
In pay? What even childhood gave!
I have been dedicate from youth.
Before my God I speak the truth!"

40

Beyond this, there is little obviously self-picturing.

Six French Poets appeared in 1915, hailed by the utter praise of William Lyon Phelps, Clement K. Shorter, and many more. *Men, Women and Ghosts* came out the succeeding year, to a chorus of applause ranging from *The Atlantic Monthly* to *Reedy's Mirror*. The poet herself is pictured as the Lady Eunice of *Pickthorn Manor*:

> Then a spell
> Of conscience sent her through the orchard spying
> Upon the gardeners. Were their tools about?
> Were any branches broken? Had the weeds
> Been duly taken out
> Under the 'spaliered pears, and were these lying
> Nailed snug against the sunny bricks and drying
> Their leaves and satisfying all their needs?
> She picked a stone up with a little pout,
> Stones looked so ill in well-kept flower-borders.

Spring Day gives her daily ritual in detail. *The Bath* comes first:

> Little spots of sunshine lie on the surface of the water and dance, dance, and their reflections wobble deliciously over the ceiling; a stir of my

finger sets them whirring, reeling. I move a
foot, and the planes of light in the water jar. I
lie back and laugh, and let the green-white
water, the sun-flawed beryl water, flow over me.

Then come the breakfast table, the walk, mid-
day, afternoon, night, and sleep. This is followed by the impressionistic *The Dinner-Party*.
With the *Fish* course we get:

"So . . ." they said,
With their wine-glasses delicately poised,
Mocking at the thing they cannot understand.

"So . . ." they said again,
Amused and insolent.
The silver on the table glittered,
And the red wine in the glasses
Seemed the blood I had wasted
In a foolish cause.

Game shows her passionate subconscious battling
against the sneers of "the gentleman with the
grey-and-black whiskers." Drawing-room, cof-
fee, talk:

They took dead men's souls
And pinned them on their breasts for orna-
        ment. . . .
And I took a green liqueur from a servant
So that he might come near me
And give me the comfort of a living thing.

42

AMY LOWELL

When the guests leave at eleven o'clock, she
bruises her hands against the pointed bars of the
railings; and, when she wakes to feel them ach-
ing, she laughs,

>   For only living flesh can suffer.

Evidently all was not inward peace in Sevenels.
Mockery, sneers, mental death—these were some
of the things she felt that she encountered from
those allowed to sesame her great suave doors.
It is easy to envy the opulent: and they do not
find it hard to envy the un-Atlased poor.

Tendencies in Modern American Poetry was
published in 1917, the first full length study of
the American poetic renascence: Randolph
Bourne and O. W. Firkins were two among
many who lauded it. The next year, it was the
four long "polyphonic prose" studies called *Can
Grande's Castle,* confessedly a book made from
books, rather than from life: John Livingston
Lowes and many another noted critic attested
their belief in its outstanding excellencies. The
next year saw *Pictures of the Floating World,*
with an even more insistent pæan of praise from
many quarters. We see her here at her domes-
tic arts:

When I have baked white cakes
And grated green almonds to spread upon them;
When I have picked the green crowns from the
      strawberries
And piled them, cone-pointed, in a blue and
      yellow platter;
When I have smoothed the seam of the linen I
      have been working,
What then?
Tomorrow it will be the same.

There is an elaborate account of *Planning the Garden,* and more of the supervision of the orchard in *Dog-Days:*

> "Tie back this branch," I say. . . .
> And I call to the man beneath,
> "Tie back that branch."

Winky and *Chopin* chronicle her reactions to her cat:

> Shall I choke you, Cat,
> Or kiss you?
> Really I do not know.

We had her killing her sheep dogs; this is another instance of the sadism that we expected to find. There will be more. Of Chopin, she said to her cat:

44

AMY LOWELL

First this,
Then spitting blood.
Music quenched in blood, . . .
"I cannot send you the manuscripts, as they are
    not yet finished.
I have been ill as a dog.
My illness has had a pernicious effect on the Pre-
    ludes
Which you will receive God knows when."
He bore it.

There is an overtone of the poet holding herself
by inner force to a harsh routine, in spite of
illness.

Legends, after a lapse of two years, was wel-
comed as her best volume, as prior volumes had
been. The same year saw the publication of
Fir Flower Tablets, poems translated from the
Chinese by Florence Ayscough, and rendered in
English verse by Miss Lowell. 1922 saw *A
Critical Fable*, published anonymously, with the
authorship later admitted by Miss Lowell.
Three years afterwards came the two volumes of
her *John Keats:* and, the same year, the posthumous *What's O'Clock*. The clock had been
stopped, before this appeared.

No contemporary poet has had such an ample
acceptance from the critics whose nod is great

in the public eye. Miss Lowell was not in the first two Braithwaite anthologies of magazine verse. Yet between the first issue and that of 1925, she was represented by thirty-three poems, to ten less for Edwin Arlington Robinson, thirteen by Robert Frost, and eleven by Vachel Lindsay. Her poems occupied a hundred and nine pages; Robinson's, forty-two; Frost's, twenty-six; Lindsay's, fifty. During that time she appeared in magazines listed by Mr. Braithwaite a hundred and forty-eight times; Robinson, thirty-nine times; Frost, thirty-six; Lindsay, twenty-eight. These statistics mean nothing beyond the fact that she was widely accepted, and represented more amply than any other prominent American poet. In Louis Untermeyer's two studies of current poetry, she stood roughly on a parity with the three singers mentioned, a page or so behind in each instance. In Miss Monroe's collection, she had more poems than any of the others, and more pages than any but Lindsay. In Marguerite Wilkinson's *New Voices*, she had equal length with Lindsay, and more than the others. She has had every opportunity to have her work known to America. Her wealth and her vigor saw to this. If America ultimately is deaf to her, it will not be for lack of ample opportunity to know her verse. The crescent bitterness that followed Poe's last days and after, the withering ostracism that met Whitman, were not hers: she was given the center window to display her wares.

In many forms public recognition came to her. Without a college education herself, she was the recipient of an honorary degree from Baylor University in 1920; she was Phi Beta Kappa poet at Tufts in 1918, and at Columbia in 1920; she gave a lecture course at the Brooklyn Institute of Arts and Sciences during 1917 and 1918; was Yale's Francis Bergen Foundation lecturer in 1921, and the Marshall Woods lecturer at Brown the same year. Louis Untermeyer, in his *New Era in American Poetry* (1919) summarizes her:

A female Roosevelt among the Parnassians. . . . But it is as an experimenter that she is most arresting. . . . No one but Masefield can surpass Miss Lowell when she is telling a narrative. . . . If Miss Lowell has done nothing else, she has enriched English as well as American literature with a new and variable medium of expression.

In his *American Poetry since 1900* (1923), a

47

"volume . . . changed in substance as well as in name" and written after "the six years that have elapsed since *The New Era* was constructed," the same critic, with much of Miss Lowell's maturest work added to the store subject to his judgment, came to this epitomizing estimate of her achievements:

A female Roosevelt among the Parnassians. . . . But it is as an experimenter that she is most arresting. . . . No one but Masefield can surpass Miss Lowell when she is telling a narrative. . . . If Miss Lowell has done nothing else, she has enriched English as well as American literature with a new and variable medium of expression.

She must have forgiven the pleonasm in "telling a narrative," in her pleasure at the constant tribute. John Livingston Lowes, in general as clear-thinking a critic as America has produced, in his *Convention and Revolt in Poetry,* calls Miss Lowell:

The most modern of the moderns. . . . The achievement in *Can Grande's Castle* itself challenges, through its vividness and contagious zest in life and color, an unreluctant admiration. . . . It is not, unless I am very much mistaken, the elements of rhyme and metre in *Can Grande's Castle* which give to it its rare union of vigor and deftness, precision and flexibility, imaginative grasp and clarity of detail. Its *formal* achievement lies rather, as I see it, in a remarkable extension of the potentialities latent in the movement of free verse.

Of her *Pictures of the Floating World* the same critic wrote:

The beauty that knocks at the gates of the senses lies on page after page with a clarity and an almost radiant succinctness for which I know few parallels. . . . Surpassing and (I think) enduring beauty.

This was his public opinion; although his private evaluation, as expressed to me and others, veered somewhat.

W. Bryher, in an ante-mortem eulogy entitled *Amy Lowell: A Critical Appreciation*, published in London in 1918, was far more rhapsodic than either of these. She describes her discovery of her work thus, *Men, Women, and Ghosts* being the book especially in mind:

I had stumbled into a freshness of vision denied so long that it had become a myth. To believe loveliness to be at point of death and find she was but sleeping—to falter upon her in the stir of her early wakefulness and touch the fluttering petals as they slip from her unused arms, is to be admitted to a share of her rediscovery of morning, to become tinged one's self with the dropping eagerness of dawn.

Of *Can Grande's Castle,* she adjudged:

Not since the Elizabethans has such a mastery of words been reached in English.

Of the New England narratives in the former book, her dictum is:

Why is it, after reading *Reaping* . . . or *Number 3 on the Docket* . . . Frost's poems, beautiful as they are, seem so inadequate?

It seems a pity to puncture such an opaline illusion: it is enough to wonder if Miss Lowell herself could have agreed with this frabjous bit of rodomontade. It is much as if she had said that nature's horizons of magnificence seem inadequate after encountering the pictorial tabloid newspapers. Of *Towns in Colour* in the same volume, she wrote:

I am dumbed with admiration as I read these poems.

We can only applaud the effect of the perusal. Theodore Maynard, a far less effusive and

50

more discriminating critic than the last, in his *Our Best Poets* (1922) reaches a different verdict. Of her use of Japanese sources he says:

This tendency has made Miss Lowell grow more and more metallic. . . . There are many disquieting signs of failing strength in Miss Lowell's prolific pen. It is a weakness when she has to rely upon brilliance instead of upon life.

We have had this criticism before, in portraits of her by her friends. He continues,

When she allows herself to be natural for a moment she is obliged to *camouflage,* as, in her pretty pieces about flowers and trees, the triteness of her theme. Further and further afield she wanders, her intellect more and more on edge, her imagination strained to the limit—looking for something to write about. Her predilection for *tour de force* is ominous. She falls back upon "Polyphonic Prose"—a literary "stunt" if ever there was one!

With less astuteness he writes,

All her books have prefatory explanations; and all the poems in them are obviously written to sustain a thesis.

This is at best half truth. The compulsion to write poetry rarely comes from any esthetic tenet; it comes from an insistent inner urge to bare one's soul to the moon. As to the manner of utterance, there is more ground for holding, superficially at least, that some pre-attained thesis determined it: yet in most cases the poems are written first, and the thesis tardily arrived at, in an endeavor to explain the music or to defend its flaws.

An interesting sidelight upon the state of popular acceptance of Miss Lowell's work is furnished by the critical reception to my *Poets of America* (1925). The summary of its attitude toward her was:

On the technical side, Miss Lowell is a glittering craftsman, lacking the genius of those who unerringly chose the patterns and tunes suitable to their words. . . . On the side of content, she fails more often; it is rare that she evokes in the mature mind that emotional response

which comes from poetry.

She is the brilliant failure in modern poetry: a polyphonic Joshua leading a crew, with a strong bedlam contingent, seven times seven seven times round and round about the walls of the poetic Jericho, which disobligingly fails to fall at her trumpet blast. It is a trumpet which she affects; and it peals less than it bleats.

The volume met with an oddly mixed reception. Two thirds of the reviews accepted it fervidly: one third were acidly hostile: none was tepid. Those who disliked it divided themselves into two definite groups: the ones who were offended at the chapter *The Waste Land,* with its dispraise of the tendency toward sham insanity in T. S. Eliot, E. E. Cummings, Maxwell Bodenheim, and others among the less felicitous experimenters; and those who disagreed hectically with the modicum of discerning depreciation mingled with the ample praise given to Edna St. Vincent Millay and Elinor Wylie. There was no single voice raised, in the two hundred or more reviews of the book, against the judgment publicly passed upon Amy Lowell. This is no dumb fact in itself.

Miss Lowell's will provided that her estate, more than three quarters of a million dollars, should go, after the death of her companion, Mrs. Ada Russell, toward encouraging poetry in the United States, in Miss Lowell's own way.

This will ultimately include a travelling scholarship bestowed upon some poet of American birth. The first posthumous volume of her work has appeared, and there may be others to follow. Meanwhile, we have much to go on, in surveying her product and her message.

III

A ROOSEVELT AMONG PARNASSIANS

In evaluating Amy Lowell as a poet, much gainless argument may be avoided, if we begin with a substructure of definition. Disputes may be divided, as a rule, into one class: those based upon diverse conceptions of the words and phrases involved. The word *poetry* has, in general, a twofold usage. It is used loosely to describe any writing which evokes the emotional response found in great poetry (in the stricter sense); and, by extension of this broader usage, to describe the same emotional response evoked by something other than writing. In the stricter, more accurate sense, poetry is the word used to name that fine art whose emotional appeal is evoked by the use of musical words, or words arranged in a rhythm differing from the rhythm of prose. In the first loose sense, Lincoln's *Gettysburg Speech* and much of our finest prose is called poetry: an unobjectional usage, if it be understood that strict language has been replaced by a lax vocabulary. Indeed, the address mentioned, and much that passes for prose, may be found to be poetry, if its rhythm is accurately studied. But this will not alter the definition which we will soon arrive at: it will merely mean that some excellent examples of poetry have been written and greeted mistakenly as prose.

Most definitions of poetry are sadly wanting in intellectual clarity. The dictionary defines it, on the technical side, as requiring (1) "musical and moving words," or (2) "usually though not necessarily arranged in the form of measured verse or numbers." The first description here is inadequate. All words are "musical": the crisp *Connecticut* no less than the mellow *magnolia*. The northern ear, accustomed to explosive speech in crisp air, may find the former the more musical. If musical groups of words are intended, the same criticism applies. The finest prose has a music no less stirring than great poetry. Again, all words are in potentiality, or actually, moving: even if they stir only to boredom. The second offered description, containing "usually," of course fails, since the use of the adverb permitting exceptions rules it out as a definition. The dictionary, then, leaves us in the air, with no more support than the melted wings of Icarus.

Macaulay, in his essay on Milton, gets no closer than in his statement that poetry does in words "what the painter does by means of colours." So may prose. Matthew Arnold grants to poetry—

the power of so dealing with things as to awaken in us a wonderfully full, new, and intimate sense of them, and of our relations to them.

Good prose does as much. Fabre's *The Life of the Spider*, Thomas Beer's *Stephen Crane*, are not poetry, and yet they precisely satisfy Arnold's dictum. Samuel Johnson is no nearer:

The essence of poetry is invention: such invention as, by producing something unexpected, surprises and delights.

Many a good detective or adventure story does as much. Coleridge is further astray, when he writes:

Poetry is not the proper antithesis to prose, but to science. Poetry is opposed to science, and prose to metre. . . . The proper and immediate object of science is the acquirement or communication of truth; the proper immediate object of poetry is the communication of immediate pleasure.

Coleridge, in thus using *antithesis,* makes the strange implication that truth and pleasure are antithetical, opposite, mutually exclusive: that the "acquirement or communication of truth" excludes pleasure, which is directly contrary to what psychology establishes. There is definite pleasure in the acquirement of truth, and in the communication of it. Science is ordered knowledge and hypothesis: its opposite is disordered knowledge and hypotheses, or statements contrary to knowledge. Prose rhythm, not prose, is opposed to poetic rhythm, a wider thing than metre; poetry is opposed to prose, in a sense, at least, that day is opposed to night. Opposition is not the right word here, if we are captious; day and night are complements describing duration with and without sunlight; prose and poetry are complements describing verbal expression with and without a regularity of rhythm, as we shall see. Even this differentiation is not yet complete.

The *Britannica* includes in its definition

"rhythmical in movement": this, and the other elements it offers, are as true of prose.

Which leaves us where we began.

Ruskin made a better start than any of these. To paraphrase his definition, poetry is the expression in musical words of thoughts which appeal to the noble emotions or their opposites. We have already indicated that "musical words" is too vague. The "appeal to the noble emotions or their opposites" excludes mere verse, such as much of Mother Goose and an infinitude of platitudinous rhymes. The "musical words" must be replaced by a more accurate phrase, giving the technical difference between prose and poetry,—defining the way that poetic rhythm differs from prose rhythm. For technically we can pass judgment upon prose and poetry as accurately as a jeweller weighing diamond dust or an astronomer weighing stardust; with the final reservation that the actual dividing line between prose and poetic rhythm is for each critic, which means each reader or listener, to arrive at for himself. The point of difference is this: the rhythm of prose tends toward variety; that of poetry, toward uniformity. We would then define:

Poetry is the expression of thoughts which awake the noble emotions or their opposites, in words whose rhythm tends toward uniformity, rather than variety.

As to content, the test is subjective: does the alleged poem awake in you the noble emotions, or their opposites? Whatever your answer is, it determines whether the particular passage is poetry or mere verse, to you. You may find all poetry in *Paradise Lost,* or in Col. D. Streamer's memorable quatrain,

> In the drinking-well
> (Which the plumber built her)
> Aunt Eliza fell.
> We must buy a filter.

The consensus of opinions, over a long stretch of time, establishes those whom the race regards as poets. As for technique, the matter may be tested by scansion, with the final differentiating point or zone between prose and poetic rhythms determined by each critic, reader, or listener. To me, Whitman's *Out of the Cradle Endlessly Rocking* is indubitably poetry; to me, most of Whitman is technically verse, although some of it sags far below the test of poetic content. To you, the *Elegy Written in a Country*

AMY LOWELL

Churchyard may mark the rhythmical limit of poetry: in which case, you will exclude most of Shakespeare, and a wealth of other material generally accepted as poetic. There is less a dividing point than a twilight zone, where the product may be regarded either as prose rhythm or poetic rhythm, and may, even with you, alter in your judgment from day to day. Definition can only be from the center, not from the circumference: noon is day, midnight is night, and twilight is both, either, or neither, as you choose to regard it. The rhythm of the typical newspaper story is prose rhythm; the rhythm of *Take, O Take Those Lips Away* is indubitably poetic. Between these two you must place your own stakes, both as to rhythm and as to the emotional effect of the matter of the product.

With this understanding, then, let us proceed to Miss Lowell's first volume, *A Dome of Many-Coloured Glass*. For all that it may testify later as to the poet's personality and problems, it is technically a surprisingly unpromising failure. It fails first from its insensitivity to the modern attitude toward the poetic vocabulary—an attitude found in Whitman's pronunciamento,

61

I had great trouble in leaving out the "stock" poetical touches, but succeeded at last.

Soon enough Miss Lowell was to shout her assent to this, in the first item of the Imagist credo:

1. To use the language of common speech, but to employ always the exact word.

She expands this, in *Tendencies,*

The language of common speech means a diction which carefully excludes inversions, and the *clichés* of the old poetic jargon.

Cliché she explains as a phrase in common use, not peculiar to the author; including old, faded expressions like "battlemented clouds" and "mountainous seas."

Among the *clichés,* rubber-stamp poeticism, or stock poetical touches in this first volume are *kissing breeze, savage ruth, 'twas a dream, freighted with hope, like to, wafts of rich perfume, scream for very joy, I am fain, opaline gates of the Castle of Dream, Nature's tender ministries, Thou yellow trumpeter of laggard spring* (of a daffodil). These are only the outstanding offenses. Edwin Arlington Robinson, since 1896, sixteen years before, had been avoiding all such phrases. As to inversions, there are many more than a dozen in the volume, such as *valleys deep, to ride I am fain* and *eggs a score* on the same page, and so on. As to the obsolescent or obsolete vocabulary, we have *athwart, dole, thee, employ* (for employment), *a-slumber, fraught, o'erhung, mart, 'tis, 'twas, standest*, and so thuddingly on. The poem *Mirage*, in two successive lines, refers to the same person as you and thee—an ungrammatical jumbling of pronouns. In *A Japanese Wood-Carving*, midway of the poem, we have another common grammatical error of Miss Lowell's, where two phrases, *Now diving quickly* . . . *Now flying up* . . . appear punctuated as if they were sentences.

The verses at times sag into an unbelievable fragility, *concetti* typical only of the perdurably inferior among magazine versifiers:

Oh! to be a flower
  Nodding in the sun,
Bending, then upspringing
  As the breezes run;
Holding up
  A scent-brimmed cup
    Full of summer's fragrance to the summer
      sun.

63

Or again,

> You came to me bearing bright roses,
>   Red like the wine of your heart;
> You twisted them into a garland
>   To set me apart from the mart.
> Red roses to crown me your lover,
>   And I walk aureoled and apart.

Or again,
>   Life is a stream
>   On which we strew
>   Petal by petal the flower of our heart.

At times the titles, *Dipsa, Hora Stellatrix, Teatro Bambino, Crépuscule du Matin,* are foreign tags flaunting an erudition desired rather than attained. All in all, the volume was an inauspicious start. There was slim newspaper praise; the ramparts of academic acceptance, the siege camps of the young insurgents, were alike unstirred. And so Miss Lowell betook herself to London and the Imagists, and threw in her lot with the extreme left. The cry arose,

> Ezra Pound and Amy Lowell,
> Chant we, New Year's Day to Noel:
> Amy Lowell, Ezra Pound,
> Lead us, on Art's battleground!

AMY LOWELL

Like a knife in the surprised ribs of a nodding poetical public came the volume *Sword Blades and Poppy Seed*: Miss Lowell was off at last!

She gives us a good text for the present study, in her intransigent, gladiatorial preface:

A work of beauty which cannot stand an intimate examination is a poor and jerry-built thing.

An intimate examination for *clichés* is not encouraging, as to the progress of her art. *Into the evening straight I went, took no note, golden flame's desire, mortal harms, harlequin sheen, Lethean dreams, I have been dedicate, stood at stare, make shift, slumbrous, adrift, aright, 'twas 'twixt, aslant, broideries, bestud, poesy, impearled, ilk, shotted, a'mass,* together with accented last syllables on *winged* and *perfumed*, a half dozen or so inversions—these are not promising. This is not surface criticism: this goes to the root of adequate poetic technique. The Imagists were right in saying that poetry must use the language of common speech. For common speech ranges from the raciest slang to the measured and weighed utterance of the land's best brains: and both have their place in poetry. But common speech avoids dead language, including many words in the vocabulary of a Shakespeare, a Keats, a Spenser, a Chaucer. It is a hallmark of the mediocre poet to mistake the archaism or obsolete word or phrase as the thing that gives vitality and poetic worth to Keats and Chaucer. Whereupon the mediocre poet sticks the dead words and phrases, with a proud flourish, into his leaden verses, and triumphantly points to them as proof that he has written poetry: for are they not found in great poetry of the past? All other things being equal, the greatest poet is he who most nearly catches the living speech. Distinguished users of it, among our contemporaries, are Robinson, Frost, Lindsay, Sandburg, Elinor Wylie. Certain poets, who use at times a dead vocabulary through ignorance of this critical generalization and the reason behind it, may still merit high praise, if their musty vocabulary is used sparingly, and is not integral to the work. Rose O'Neill is an outstanding example of this: but her poeticisms are never the crowns of her work; they are at best its misdemeanors.

Similar weakness is revealed by Miss Lowell's rhyme, *life, strife*. Such a rhyme is as clearly a part of the old poetic jargon, as *breeze, trees;*

kiss, bliss; love, dove; and other galled and de-
crepit rhyming jades. Let me grant that a use
original enough may salvage even such a pair
of words; let me grant that a rhyme, once on
every pen, may have been interred so long that
its exhumation adds to the living tools of poetry.
The modern usage, again to increase the tools of
poetry, tends rather to such melodious near-
rhymes or assonances as *worry, bury; withered,*
gathered; cluttered, spattered; quarrel, laurel;
hunters, winter's; valleys, bellies, all from Miss
Millay's *The Poet and His Book.* Two usages in
the same poem, *cupboard, upward; homely,*
lonely, are more questionable, the second especially because it is a favorite false rhyme of
Village Miltonlings ignorant of accurate ryhme.
Yet even at that, these are infinitely preferable
to the *love-dove* type.

A skilful use of *clichés* may be essential to a
poem definitely of a period. Yet Robinson's
Merlin, his greatest sustained achievement, uses
predominantly a modern vocabulary, and this is
only one of the many ways in which it outshines
the pallidity of Tennyson's *Idylls of the King,*
where the older speech is retained. As for Miss
Lowell, in this volume, it is at least true that, for

all her ancient jargon, there is a bellicose vigor throughout that is far from musty, and is in direct contrast to the earlier book. She has stepped ahead, from her very opening:

> A drifting, April, twilight sky,
> A wind which blew the puddles dry,
> And slapped the river into waves
> That ran and hid among the staves
> Of an old wharf.

"All day," she says,

> My thoughts had lain as dead,
> Unborn and bursting in my head.
> From time to time I wrote a word
> Which lines and circles overscored.
> My table seemed a graveyard, full
> Of coffins waiting burial.

The poet, in this opening poem, encounters "Ephraim Bard. Dealer in Words," who tells her, "All books are either dreams or swords"— a pleasant enough epigram, which might be stretched toward acceptance as fanciful truth. The poet leaves the shop at length, equipped with varied seeds to induce dreams, and the finest swords in the shop. The poet in question is, of course, Miss Lowell: it is hardly necessary to point out that she is not intrinsically modest as to her own equipment. Her attitude here is admirable, rather than the reverse: if the poet does not believe in his or her own product, the world shows a cynical tendency to agree at once with the self-depreciation. Among the "sword blades" of the volume is *The Cyclists,*

> Spread on the roadway,
> With open-blown jackets,
> Like black, soaring pinions,
> They swoop down the hillside,
>   The Cyclists.
>
> Seeming dark-plumaged
> Birds, after carrion,
> Careening and circling,
> Over the dying
>   Of England.

The verse is inoffensive enough, as verse goes; but the meaning of it is more than trifling. A moment's glimpse might cause one to regard cyclists as carrion birds: but really, you know, cyclists are awf'ly harmless chaps, and all that. She gives us a flashed image of no great value rigidified into a tepid perpetuity, and that is all. *The Captured Goddess* shows Miss Lowell's use of what she preferred to call "cadenced verse" rather than "free verse" or polyrhythmic verse:

Over the housetops,
Above the rotating chimney pots,
I have seen a shiver of amethyst,
And blue and cinnamon have flickered
A moment,
At the far end of a dusty street.

Through sheeted rain
Has come a lustre of crimson,
And I have watched moonbeams
Hushed by a film of palest green.

It was her wings,
Goddess!
Who stepped over the clouds,
And laid her rainbow feathers
Aslant on the currents of the air.

As verse, this astringent pattern is gently pleasing. There are vague spots, and a multitude of
colors; but all in all it pleases rather than the
reverse. It gives the impression, however, of
a vision overly objective; and though the progress of the poem negatives this somewhat, the
abiding impression is that there is nothing here
to conscript superlatives, or even permit them to
volunteer. There is music here, pleasing music;
but, to me at least, there is the lack of that ultimate word music, that flawless fusing of thought
to phrase, that makes the enduring altitude of

A savage place! as holy and enchanted
As e'er beneath a waning moon was haunted
By woman wailing for her demon lover;

or,

O wild West Wind, thou breath of Autumn's
    being,
Thou, from whose unseen presence the dead
    leaves
Are driven, like ghosts from an enchanter
    fleeing,

Yellow, and black, and pale, and hectic red,
Pestilence-stricken multitudes;

or,

Earth of shine and dark mottling the tide of the
    river!
Earth of the limpid grey of clouds brighter and
    clearer for my sake!
Far-swooping elbow'd earth—rich apple-blos-
    som'd earth!
Smile, for your lover comes;

or,

Part of a moon was falling down the west,
Dragging the whole sky with it to the hills.
Its light poured softly in her lap.

From this we may grant her grace, in her own

way, rather than greatness. She is charmingly clever in *Astigmatism*, the etching of Ezra Pound; but cleverness is at best a ground flight of poetry. *The Coal Picker*, who sees

> A Spanish castle old,
> With silver steps and paths of gold.
> From myrtle bowers comes the plash
> Of fountains, and the emerald flash
> Of parrots in the orange trees,
> Whose blossoms pasture humming bees,

is amazingly out of drawing. Miss Lowell has never been a coal picker, as far as the records indicate, and it did not need this poem to establish that fact. *A Tale of Starvation* weds an adequate theme to the most incongruous Mother Goose jingle of a tune:

> And so it happened from day to day
>   The old man fed his life
> On the beauty of his vase, on its perfect shape,
>   And his soul forgot its former strife.

We intend no libel to Mother Goose, and perhaps should withdraw Miss Lowell's amiable predecessor's name. The ineptitude here dumbs me, to use the classic locution of Bryher.

Among the *Poppy Seeds* are several narratives. *The Great Adventure of Max Breuck* is an

astonishing melodrama, with a villainous money-
lender who has forced a promise of marriage
from his debtor's daughter; a loving solicitor
who weds a girl after two years of implicit woo-
ing; then—Pouf!—the discovery that the whole
incident is a drug-induced dream, with no girl,
no money-lender, no father-debtor: concluding
with the suicide of the duped solicitor,—all told
in verse essentially mediocre. *After Hearing a
Waltz by Bartok* is a hysterical study of murder:

But why did I kill him? Why? Why?
  In the small, gilded room, near the stair?
My ears rack and throb with his cry,
  And his eyes goggle under his hair,
  As my fingers sink into the fair
White skin of his throat. It was I! . . .

One! Two! Three! Give me air! Oh! My
      God!
  One! Two! Three! I am drowning in
      slime!
One! Two! Three! And his corpse, like a
      clod,
  Beats me into a jelly! The chime,
  One! Two! Three! And his dead legs
      keep time.
Air! Give me air! Air! My God!

This may establish a sprint exclamation point record—twenty-one to a six line stanza. There is not a Sweet Singer of Lake Passamaquoddy who would not be laughed out of court for such shoddy work. It is difficult to refuse an enthusiastic compliance with the final exhortation. She has not yet established her right to stand just behind Masefield as a narrative poet.

It is difficult to praise a phrase like,

> The great sun hung,
> A navel for the curving sky.

Its fault is an unnecessary incongruity in the context, and a lack of beauty, both in phrasing and vision. The most surprising thing about the volume, in view of the critical acceptance it received, is that there is not one poem outstanding which succeeds as a whole: which lingers in the memory, and invites the reader to return to it for its poetic quality.

Men, Women and Ghosts is a finer volume. The *clichés* have all but vanished—a negative merit. The opening poem, *Patterns,* is by all odds her most popular product; and, with the possible exception of one or two other poems, her most poetic product. In it, she has mastered her medium almost completely:

74

AMY LOWELL

I walk down the garden paths,
And all the daffodils
Are blowing, and the bright blue squills.
I walk down the patterned garden-paths
In my stiff brocaded gown.
With my powdered hair and jewelled fan,
I too am a rare
Pattern.   As I wander down
The garden paths.

Here we must pause.   The break introduced by
"As" is not only ungrammatical, but it is un-
musical, adds nothing to the picture, and is a
definite let-down.   The tenth and eighteenth
lines in stanza two mark similar crudities; the
last line of the third stanza is another instance.
Consider this beauty:

I would be the pink and silver as I ran along the
    paths,
And he would stumble after
Bewildered by my laughter.

This lovely phrase is followed by an unaiding
dissonance:

I should see the sun flashing from his sword-hilt
    and the buckles on his shoes.

Once more in this stanza, twice in the one following, occurs the break in the music and the

tension. The stanza next to the last is definitely weaker than the others: then comes a lovely stretch—

In Summer and in Winter I shall walk
Up and down
The patterned garden-paths
In my stiff, brocaded gown.
The squills and daffodils
Will give place to pillared roses, and to asters,
      and to snow.

I must pause to express utter delight in the exquisite couplet just quoted. Here we have poetry, inevitable in music, haunting in its evocation of the slow surge of beauty toward its hour of sleep. In dreadful contrast, the two lines before the final couplet are as sodden as a mired path.

The poem, in spite of its flaws, succeeds: it is a period picture out of the poet's heart, giving a full sense of the tragedy of love inconsummate. The theme is poignant; and the emotion evoked overrules immediate "intimate examination," to use Miss Lowell's phrase. When, in the cool aftermath, the poem is studied, it must be confessed that its worth remains as a dramatic monolog; and that the attitude of the woman is

AMY LOWELL

emotional rather than intellectual. For love,
and marriage, are as much patterns as war is.
Of its kind, the poem is excellent. A slightly
keener ear for word music would have elided
the flaws, and made it infinitely surer of man's
eternity.

Pickthorn Manor, a long narrative of adultery
with a melodrama finale ending:

In perfect quietness they sleep, remote
In the green, rippled twilight. Death has smote
  Them to perpetual oneness who were twain.

is in general verse fairly adequate, but hardly
distinguished; and the solecism, "has smote," for
"has smitten," while excusable on the old sham
plea of poetic license, is not what an artist in
words would have allowed to remain. The
weakness of such a narrative is silhouetted
blackly against a bright sunrise, when it is compared with the average work of Masefield,
Robinson, Chesterton, Frost, and several other
contemporaries. *The Cremona Violin* is experimental, in that it seeks to catch the music of the
strings in rippling free verse, interspersed
throughout the groups of Chaucerian stanzas:

She leans upon the beating, throbbing
Music. Laughing, sobbing,

77

Feet gliding after sliding feet;
His—hers—
The ballroom blurs—
She feels the air
Lifting her hair,
And the lapping of water on the stone stair.
He is there!   He is there!

It is an admirable effort.   Whether it has per-
manence is another matter; the bulk of it seems
too verbosely tenuous to persist. *A Roxbury
Garden* attempts to catch in quick lines the
rolling of a hoop:

Turn, hoop,
Burn hoop,
Twist and twine,
Hoop of mine.
Flash along,
Leap along,
Right at the sun.
Run, hoop, run.

Again, she has tried to net a new note into
poetry: but the effect is inconsequential and
interesting, rather than obviously enduring.
We will leave her experiments with "polyphonic
prose" until we reach the next volume. *1777*
is a glittering study in contrasts; the quality of
glitter is becoming Miss Lowell's distinguishing

mark. And glitter, whatever its worth, evokes amazement rather than a deeper emotion. *The Hammers* glitters magnificently; at times its technique is obviously and beyond argument that of prose; yet Homer, Shakespeare, Whitman sagged at times, without defeating their right to the title of poet. *A Ballad ʃ Footmen*, among the war poems, is an absurd nursery jingle again, worse than poor propaganda verse:

Now what in the name of the sun and the stars
Is the meaning of this most unholy of wars?

Do men find life so full of humour and joy
That for want of excitement they smash up the
    toy?

The inclusion of such a piece of execrable thinking and execrable rhythm indicates a depressing lack of self-critical ability.

The section entitled *The Overgrown Pasture* (which, you may recall, dumbed Bryher) is an attempt to catch some of the essence of backland New England in colloquial cadenced verse, to use Miss Lowell's phrase. As sheer stories, the three monologs are worth telling. *The Reaping* reports how a wife, neglected by her husband, commits adultery, confesses it, and is proud of it; *Off the Turnpike* tells of a widow's hallucination of finding a dead hand, without a body, in her garden; *Nunber 3 on the Docket*, tells how a wife, driven insane by her husband's silence, murdered him with his logging ax. As tragic recitations, in prose, these would be effective: it is doubtful if, technically, they can be yanked in any way under the category of poetry. Take the opening of the first:

You want to know what's the matter with me,
    do yer?
My! ain't men blinder'n moles?
It ain't nothin' new, be sure o' that.
Why, ef you'd had eyes you'd ha' seed
Me changin' under your very nose,
Each day a little diff'rent.
But you never see nothin', you don't.

Let us read this as the prose that its rhythm indicates it is:

    You want to know what's the matter with me, do yer? My! ain't men blinder'n moles? It ain't nothin' new, be sure o' that. Why, ef you'd had eyes you'd ha' seed me changin' under your very nose, each day a little diff'rent. But you never see nothin', you don't.

The most careful scansion fails to indicate anything approaching a poetic rhythm here: the most sympathetic reading aloud fails to discover the underlying tendency toward uniformity. It can be read with poetic rhythm, by adding to it what it does not contain: certain artificial pauses, to take the place of omitted syllables, both accented and unaccented. Any prose may be so set to music, that the holds and pauses give it a regularity not inherent in it. Yet it remains essentially prose: and this is at least in the twilight zone, on the prose side. Take the opening of *The Grocery*, cast in the appropriate prose form:

"Hullo, Alice!"

"Hullo, Leon!"

"Say, Alice, gi' me a couple o' them two for five cigars, will yer?"

"Where's your nickel?"

"My! Ain't you close! Can't trust a feller, can yer."

"Trust you! Why what you owe this store would set you up in business. I can't think why Father 'lows it."

"Yer Father's a sight more neighborly than you be. That's a fact. Besides, he knows I got a vote."

"A vote! Oh, yes, you got a vote! A lot o' good the Senate'll be to Father when all his bank account has run away in credits."

This is experimental; as poetry, it is impossible. The very rhythms of spoken prose are here in many places, not lifted by emotion into such intensity that the words automatically fall into a poetic rhythm. It is a passable prose dialog.

The most eccentric experiment in the book, *Stravinsky's Three Pieces "Grotesques," for String Quartette,* consists of frayed and dishevelled prose gobbets containing such wild bits as—

Bump-e-ty-tong! Whee-e-e! Tong! The thin Spring leaves shake to the banging of shoes. Shoes beat, slap, shuffle, rap, and the nasal pipes squeal with their pigs' voices, little pigs' voices weaving among the dancers, a fine white thread linking up the dancers. Bang! Bump! Tong! Petticoats, stockings, sabots, delirium flapping its thigh-bones; . . . pigs' cries white and tenuous, white and painful, white and— Bump! Tong!

The emotion evoked in you may be the poetic one: let me reveal that it is not so with me. The rhythm is disjointed prose, in any case. It is set up as verse, in short lines: and we wonder how the most devout among the Lowellians or Eliotics can divide it into the original lining, unless guided wholly by memory.

Yet, after all, this volume contained *Patterns,* a genuine poem; three good colloquial prose monologs; and some mediocre narrative verse. *Can Grande's Castle,* which came next, is four long impressionistic tales in polyphonic prose. Of this form, Mr. Maynard says:

"Polyphonic Prose" is nothing less than a synthesis of every conceivable literary mode, ranging from bald statement to balder doggerel—a haggis pie into which innumerable ingredients are thrown at hazard.

Professor Lowes, one of the most appreciative and friendly of Miss Lowell's critics, quotes her explanation,

"Polyphonic prose" is not a prose form, although, being printed as prose, many people have found it difficult to understand this.

His comment is surprisingly frank:

But even an intelligent reader may be pardoned if he fails to understand that what is called prose and printed as prose is yet not prose. It is a little as if, your name being Schwartzkopf, and your physiognomy Teutonic, you should expect me to understand that you were Irish.

Miss Lowell, seeking to defend her pet form, says of it,

I decided to base my form upon the long, flowing cadence of oratorical prose.

From this, she says, she can shift easily to *vers libre* or metre. Her mind blinked, blind to the obvious fact that "oratorical prose" was prose, and not poetry. She uses oratorical prose, and, by the magic conjuration of calling it "polyphonic prose," expects it to become immediately "not prose," but poetry. It simply will not obey. The transmogrification does not work: Bottom remains translated into an ass.

Take the opening of *Sea-Blue and Blood-Red*:

Blue as the tip of the salvia blossom, the inverted cup of the sky arches over the sea. Up to meet it, in a flat band of glaring colour, rises the water. The sky is unspecked by clouds, but the sea is flecked with pink and white light shadows, and silver scintillations snip-snap over the tops of the waves.

This is not good prose: it is too affected, too noisily colorful, too full of inverted phrase order and febrile description: in a word, too snip-snappy. It is not poetry. It neither evokes the the emotions that poetry awakens, nor is it rhythmically poetry. It glitters, it scintillates, it burns like a gigantic fake fire-opal and clangs

"like forty-seven bands a-playing all together."
A few pages of it please by the noisy novelty,
and then the ear becomes deafened to the constant unremitting fortissimo, the eyes sting at
the painfully dazzling pyrotechnics, and the
thing is laid by in an astonished bewilderment.
There are more than two hundred pages in the
four pieces.

The flashing retelling of the relation between
Nelson and Lady Hamilton is in the spirit of the
period. *Guns as Keys: and the Great Gate
Swings* is an effective piece of writing; with the
staccato passages broken, to the reader's relief,
by passages of polyrhythmic verse. Here are
the two moods:

Across the equator and panting down to Saint
Helena, trailing smoke like a mourning veil.
Jamestown jetty, and all the officers in the ship
making at once for Longwood. Napoleon!
Ah, tales—tales—with nobody to tell them. A
bronze eagle caked by floating woodwork. A
heart burst with beating on a flat drop-curtain
of sea and sky. Nothing new but pigs in a
sty. . . .

The ladies,
Wistaria Blossom, Cloth-of-Silk, and Deep Snow,
With their ten attendants,

85

Are come to Asakusa
To gaze at peonies,
To admire crimson-carmine peonies,
To stare in admiration at bomb-shaped, white
    and sulphur peonies,
To caress with a soft finger

eight more lines of peonies. The emotion cannot come from the fragments: there is neither memorable wording in either, nor a poetic rhythm in the passages set up as prose. There is a cumulative emotional effect in the piece: as an art form, objective in character, part prose and part verse, it is interesting and stimulating. The tenor is somewhat like Carlyle's more hectic passages, with sharp overtones of criticism at times:

A locomotive in pay for a Whistler; telegraph wires buying a revolution; weights and measures and Audubon's birds in exchange for fear. Yellow monkey-men leaping out of Pandora's box, shaking the rocks of the Western coastline. Golden California bartering panic for prints. The dressing-gowns of a continent won at the cost of security.

A strange blend, attractive, unpoetic, and in the end unsatisfying. *Hedge Island* is a lesser bit, *The Bronze Horses* wider in potentialities.

Neither is as effective as the Japanese-American mish-mash. Neither is poetry. This sounds dogmatic: it is understood that I phrase an individual judgment, in the last analysis, as each reader must do for himself. If any one can accept such rhythm as poetic, it is his privilege. But it is doubtful if the world will ever swing so far toward renaming black as white. The product is not gray here, but black—the reverse of poetic rhythm. When we reach such a passage as,

Such a pounding, pummelling, pitching, pointing, piercing, pushing, pelting, poking, panting, punching, parrying, pulling, prodding, puking, piling, passing, you never did see,

I am content to leave the matter to the common sense of the readers of the strange hybrid.

Pictures of the Floating World appeared in 1919; there is again no outstanding poem in the whole volume. Much of it consists of mere objective fragments, as this *Near Kioto*:

As I crossed over the bridge of Ariwarano Nari-
    kira,
I saw that the waters were purple
With the floating leaves of maple.

87

It is probable that this is not even verse, but prose: in any case, it is too inconsequential to trouble the critic or the seeker for poetry. *De minimis Musa non curat.* After pages of this, we have a section of love poems, undistinguished in treatment, minor incidents dressed glitteringly. Then we reach *Ely Cathedral,* an acid flash of satire:

Anemic women, stupidly dressed and shod
In squeaky shoes, thump down the nave to laud
    an expurgated God.

The theme appeals to minds restive under the pricks of ritualistic religion; it is poetry of a low flight, if it earns the laurelled noun. The war poems are less stridently jingoistic than Miss Lowell's worst save one, *Phantasm of War: The Cornucopia of Red and Green Comfits,* which appeared in *The Independent,* and was reprinted by Marguerite Wilkinson in her *New Voices* with the typical comment that it is one of Miss Lowell's "greatest achievements." The handling is tawdry, the theme is one of the false bits of atrocity propaganda spread, in this case, by publicity spokesmen for the Allies, just as the German enemy was doing. The concluding poem in the volume, *To a Certain Critic,* a tribute to Keats, has been highly admired by Bryher, the English adulator. After Keats, it is tasteless fare.

Legends, appearing in 1921, has been called Miss Lowell's greatest book: as which, indeed, has not? It is a pleasure, for her sake, to chronicle that some have found some of the stories or legends superbly told: it is doubtful if this judgment will be concurred in by the future. This again is a book from books—a venial fault, merely reminding us that half of the tale-teller's task has been done for him, and that only in the telling will the creative artistic nature be revealed. Miss Lowell, as the longest poem in her first book attests, and as all who knew her have stated, was bookish, was a student for many years before her first volume appeared. We are entitled to some accuracy of detail from her, if her scholarship is even negatively satisfactory. In this book we have tigers located in Peru and loosely in North America; dates in primitive Peru; and olives in primitive Yucatan. Tigers are exclusively Asian; the American "tiger-cat," less than three feet long, is not a tiger. Dates and olives were confined

to the Old World, until long after 1492.   These
are minor matters: but a passable scholarship
would not have let them slip in.   We have
feathered arrows—

Terrible in swiftness because the feathers had not
been cut or burned to make them low.

This is the reverse of accurate, as any one con-
versant with archery knows.   For arrows used
in hunting big game, or in human warfare, as
in this poem, the feathers are wide, to give
straightness of aim; for distance shooting, where
a high trajectory is needed, the feather is nar-
rowed down to almost nothing.   Cutting or
burning the feathers would not make them low,
but would aid their high flight.   Why should
this author be familiar with archery, one might
ask?   If she is to write about archery, she must
become familiar with it: especially as she bore the
reputation of a scholar.   Again, Miss Lowell referred to "an antiquity dealer's," where the more
accurate locution would be "antique dealer's."
In a New England garden picture, the result of
two days of cold rain is that, at the end of the
second day, the clumps of flowers are "beaten
offal" and the walks are littered with "the rot-

ting stalks of headless plants." This picture is so amazingly overdrawn that it is, to all intents and purposes, wholly inaccurate. It is a hysteric exaggeration, as if the inner compulsion demanded an extreme accentuation of the truth, until it became something else.

Her artistry here is as inept as her scholarship. The climax of the ancient Peruvian fox and moon poem, told in language predominantly simple, refers to rings of

Stinging, glutinous, intorting coils of smoke,

a flareup of erudite vocabulary entirely out of the drawing. In *Many Swans*, the funeral dirge "The Nation's drum has fallen down, Beat—beat —and a double beat!" continues for three stanzas of strained and crude echoes of the refrain technique Rossetti used so acceptably. There is a passage,

> Rattle—rattle—rattle—
> Rattle—rattle—rattle—
> The Rattlers,
> The Rattlesnakes.
> Hiss-s-s-s!
> Ah-h-h!
> White Rattlesnakes,
> Green Rattlesnakes,

Black-and-yellow Rattlesnakes,
Barred like tigers.

By now, the question as to whether the passage
quoted is poetry or not approaches the monot-
onous. To the borrowed technique she adds the
nature note concerning white rattlesnakes and
green ones, and both of these have so far es-
caped our discovery. In *The Ring and the
Castle* she establishes that she can write as baldly
in rhyme as without it:

I took the ring and the bleeding finger, and sent
    a messenger swiftly forth,
An amazing gift to my Lord I sent them, in his
    lonely castle to the North.
He died, they say, at sight of my present. I
    laughed when I heard it—"Hee! Hee!
    Hee!"

An amazing gift and *Hee! Hee! Hee!* are hardly
the stuff of great poetry, or of poetry. We
must charitably overlook many phrases akin to:

    Julius, the Gardener behind
    Runs with a frothy, scarlet cud
    Oozing out of his mouth.

The catalog of ineptitudes stretches out to the
crack of doom. One more must be chronicled,
for its astounding matrix:

92

AMY LOWELL

> Antelope and buffalo,
> Threading the tall green grass they go,
> To and fro, to and fro,
> And painted Indians ride in a row,
> With arrow and bow, arrow and bow,
> Hunting the antelope, the buffalo,
> Truly they made a gallant show,
> Across the prairie's bright green flow,
> Warriors painted indigo,
> Brown antelope, black buffalo,
> Long ago.

Waiving all problems of *clichés* and general doughiness, there is something annoyingly familiar about these lines. Where has this same tune floated into the consciousness, and remained forever affixed in the reservoir of unconscious memory? And then the cue flashes up, and we turn to the White Knight's song in *Through the Looking-Glass*,

> And now, if e'er by chance I put
>   My fingers into glue,
> Or madly squeeze a right-hand foot
>   Into a left-hand shoe,
> Or if I drop upon my toe
>   A very heavy weight,
> I weep, for it reminds me so
> Of that old man I used to know—
> Whose look was mild, whose speech was slow,

93

Whose hair was whiter than the snow,
Whose face was very like a crow,
With eyes, like cinders, all aglow,
Who seemed distracted with his woe,
Who rocked his body to and fro,
And muttered mumblingly and low,
As if his mouth were full of dough,
Who snorted like a buffalo—
That summer evening long ago,
    A-sitting on a gate.

Barring Carroll's closing rhyme line, the last two rhyming words are identical: *buffalo, ago.* Lewis Carroll, in this verse for children of all ages, is a master rhymester: he rhymes twelve *o* sounds, with only one duplication. Miss Lowell, in her subsequent adult legend, in eleven *o* sounds, repeats the *-go* and *-lo* sounds each three times. This is the difference between craftsmanship and cobbling.

We need give little more time to *Legends.* The fox and moon story, and *Witch-Woman,* two out of eleven, are passable stories: the rest are melodramatic, or scrappy, or otherwise wholly ineffective. Miss Lowell has dug up new ore for some of them; but her telling is beyond the suburbs of distinguished. To liken her art to Masefield's is stultification of criticism. *Fir-*

AMY LOWELL

Flower Tablets, the translations from the Chinese, are apparently adequate renderings of what is poetry in the original. But the idioms and tunes of the two languages are so dissimilar, that the English version suffers perhaps from an over-faithfulness, in that the material is never re-created into English poetry. It is a good work-manlike book, bare of the soul spark that is poetry.

The posthumous *What's O'Clock* expands the long picture, of slim beauty and dark blemish alike. The opening poem uses the Rossetti type of refrain without artistry; the third movement of this poem sags far below the same poet's

> Lazy laughing languid Jenny,
> Fond of a kiss and fond of a guinea,

far from the Everest of poetry, but how notably better than Miss Lowell's work here! Four poems before the poem dedicated to Poe we find a poor Poesque echo. We find soggy melodrama here and there. We find the nondescript *Texas*, in formal English, containing a vulgarism as amazing as

> Terribly sweet
> The cardinals sing in the live-oak trees.

We have much that, for Miss Lowell's sake, must
be forgotten, and will be: and we find one poem
so hauntingly lovely that we marvel that the
same hand could write it and the "poor jerry-
built things" that make up the Death Valley of
the whole. *Nuit Blanche* is as affecting as the
more distinguished music of Conrad Aiken; it
is, to this ear at least, enduring poetry.

I want no horns to rouse me up tonight,
And trumpets make too clamorous a ring
To fit my mood, it is so weary white
I have no wish for doing any thing.

A music coaxed from humming strings would
     please;
Not plucked, but drawn in creeping cadences
Across a sunset wall where some Marquise
Picks a pale rose amid strange silences.

Ghostly and vaporous her gown sweeps by
The twilight dusking wall, I hear her feet
Delaying on the gravel, and a sigh,
Briefly permitted, touches the air like sleet.

And it is dusk, I hear her feet no more.
A red moon leers beyond the lily-tank.
A drunken moon ogling a sycamore,
Running long fingers down its shining flank.

AMY LOWELL

A lurching moon, as nimble as a clown,
Cuddling the flowers and trees which burn like
    glass.
Red, kissing lips, I feel you on my gown—
Kiss me, red lips, and then pass—pass.

Music, you are pitiless to-night.
And I so old, so cold, so languorously white.

It is difficult to phrase the delight that the discovery of such a poem brings.   The critic goes
to a book, not seeking its flaws and failures, but
its excellences: he is otherwise not fit to be a
critic.   If he finds the former, a sense of his
responsibility to the craft of criticism lays on
him the imperative to chronicle them, as charitably as is consonant with honesty, that others
may avoid the quickmud.   But his search is for
the latter: if a contemporary poet has failed, a
part of himself has failed likewise, since he must
regard every contemporary as part of his own
voice, the voice of the age he seeks to express.
No poet—and our discerning critic must be
that—desires to be measured beside dead Olym-
pians and living pygmies: his best can best be
evoked by a high worth around him.   From the
thin-aired plateau of the ages the low valley with
one outstanding hill is little, compared to a

rugged range whose many peaks split the clouds. We have sought to find what is enduring and worthy in Miss Lowell. We find *Patterns*, memorable, and not quite flawless; we find *Nuit Blanche*, magical and haunting; we find a persisting experimentation, lacking subtlety of ear, knowledge, or intuition; we find flaws beyond anticipation. For the slim merits our delight rises; but the abiding impression is that Miss Lowell, in verse, was less poet than celebrity.

IV

THE BROOKLINE RHADAMANTHUS

Miss Lowell, as critic, bulked as large in the public eye as in her rôle of poet. The encomiums that met her efforts in this field excelled, in sustained tone, her acclaim as poet. The six prefaces to her volumes of collected poems, the articles in periodicals, the studies of modern French poets and American tendencies, and the biographical critique of John Keats, as well as *A Critical Fable*, her anonymous child, indicate her extent and range as literary arbiter. How did she demean herself in this field?

The first preface contained this generalization:

The poet must learn his trade in the same manner, and with the same painstaking care, as the cabinet-maker.

Perhaps the poet should so learn his trade: but the crafts are essentially different. Utter knowledge of his trade, in theory and practice, would make a great cabinet-maker; utter knowledge of his art would not make more than a hack poet. A discriminating and innovating artistic sense would make a greater cabinet-maker; something of this is needed to make a poet merely acceptable, and far from great.

In this preface, Miss Lowell describes the medium, commonly called free verse or polyrhythmic verse,

I prefer to call them (many of the poems in this volume) poems in "unrhymed cadence," for that conveys their exact meaning to an English ear.

Her loose use of words appears here in the "their." She does not mean what she says: that a mere renaming of the form conveys the exact meaning of the poems to an English ear. The renaming of the form does not affect the meaning of the poems at all: it conveys, perhaps, "its" exact meaning—the meaning of the art form—to an English ear. This Miss Lowell meant to say: this she did not say. Her description of the form is no less unsatisfactory:

They differ from ordinary prose rhythms by being more curved, and containing more stress.

Both of these statements are obscure and fundamentally unhelpful. Poetic rhythm may be more curved, or less curved, than prose rhythm. In endstopped lines, as in Gray's *Elegy,* the curve is short; in this speech of Othello's it is longer:

> Had it pleas'd heaven
> To try me with affliction, had they rain'd
> All kinds of sores and shames on my bare head,
> Steep'd me in poverty to the very lips,
> Given to captivity me and my utmost hopes,
> I should have found in some place of my soul
> A drop of patience; but, alas, to make me
> A fixed figure for the time of scorn
> To point his slow unmoving finger at!
> Yet I could bear that too.

I quote from an editorial in this morning's *World:*

The Aldermen were unanimous yesterday in asking the renewal of the Rent Law. So much was expected. Neither party opposed renewal. The big task begins when the new measure is to be framed.

Assuming (the assumption most favorable to Miss Lowell's thesis) that the clause punctuation in *Othello* means separate curves, the syllables to each rhythmic phrase number 12, 13, 11, 13, 15,

26, 6. Those in the prose editorial number 24, 6, 9, 14. These are not extreme cases: the curve of poetry may be short or long, that of prose the same. Nor need either contain more stress than the other. A flowing polysyllabled poetry would contain far less stress than a staccato, short-syllabled prose. The technical difference between poetry (including polyrhythmic poetry) and prose, as to rhythm, has been indicated before: it is a question of the tendency toward uniformity or variety.

Miss Lowell's surprising ignorance of grammatical usage mars all of her critical writing. We shall, in general, omit such instances; but they are omnipresent. For instance, the third sentence in the preface to *Men, Women and Ghosts* uses the word *both* to modify three types of verse included; *both* is, of course, correctly used to refer to two, and not three, objects or ideas. The next preface insists that her polyphonic prose, named prose, printed as prose, based "upon the long, flowing cadence of oratorical prose" is "certainly not prose." The plaintiff rests. The preface to *Legends* uses the improper form *proven* for proved, and the solecism "Man is a strangely alike animal" for

AMY LOWELL

"Men are strangely alike." There are more than a dozen ungrammatical connections in this preface. As with many prefaces, this foreword is useless; what information it contains belongs to a brief appendix.

In an article on the "new poetry" in *The New York Times* for March 26, 1916, Miss Lowell reveals her queer quirks as a critic. She derives Frost from Whitman and French and English prose writers; Vachel Lindsay from Coleridge and Poe; and Browning from Matthew Arnold. This last is a remarkable discovery, inasmuch as Browning (1812–1889) antedated Arnold (1822–1888), and had published *Pauline, Paracelsus,* and *Sordello* at the ages of twenty-one, twenty-three, and twenty-eight; and Arnold's first published poem (an undergraduate production) appeared the year that the third of the Browning poems misted into print. Miss Lowell strangely saw the merit of free verse as

to give vividness when vividness is desired.

An infinitude of metric verse is as vivid as any of man's utterances. Cadence, the distinguishing mark of free verse to her, she defines as "the sense of balance"—which is as accurate as to say that the distinguishing mark of a dog is that it eats food.   She said further,

I wish that no man could expect to make a living by writing.   I wish that the magazines did not pay for contributions.

Miss Lowell's estate, at her death, was appraised at eight hundred thousand dollars.   She could afford these wishes.   The subtle influence of her wealth secured the prompt publication of her overlong volumes of collected poems.   Her six last volumes averaged 266 pages; Robinson's last seven, 144 pages; four of Vachel Lindsay's, 148 pages—these two being chosen as poets of similar productivity to Miss Lowell.

Her review of *The New Adam* in the same paper commenced:

Mr. Untermeyer is the most versatile writer in America, of that there can be no shadow of a doubt.

Yet there is.   She is more accurate in describing him as

a pleasant and suggestive critic, rather than a profound one.

Six French Poets, her first volume of criticism, was described by *La France* as

AMY LOWELL

Une très interessante étude.

I am not alone among American critics in re-
alizing my limitations in dealing with this trans-
pontic theme. Miss Lowell's preface explains
that the book consists of her Boston lectures of
1914,

rewritten and arranged for the press.

She concludes the volume on this note:

The book is done. I have not attempted any
very far-reaching criticism. My object has
been to talk a little while about a few great
figures.

The style is unostentatious and colloquial, and
as marred by lapses of grammar and word-usage
as her other critical writings. The book is interesting, its chief lack being any conveyed sense
of the sweep of movements in French poetry,
beyond the six poets mentioned. Distinguished
French scholars have said that much of its matter may be found in widely-known French
critiques.

In dealing with *Tendencies in Modern American Poetry*, published in 1917, American critics
are on surer ground. Miss Lowell is entitled to

high credit, as being first in the field. She achieved the primary survey of the modern renascence of poetry in America. While she limited her study to six poets, she gave a hint of the ones without her fold; and thus definitely became the first publicity agent for the still maturing boom in our poetry. And yet her very title, in the light of her treatment, was a misnomer. She gave three definite tendencies: the poets who wrote in the atmosphere of the breakdown of the American tradition (Robinson and Frost); the poets who wrote in the cynical chaos and despair following this (Masters and Sandburg); and the poets who wrote under "new beliefs," living upon "other planes of thought" (H. D. and John Gould Fletcher.) This is her own summary. Masters (in the original *Spoon River Anthology* and most of his earlier work) belonged definitely to the same tendency as Robinson and Frost, with a mere alteration in geography. Sandburg (as well as the predominant work of Arturo Giovanitti and much of Vachel Lindsay) tended much less toward despair than toward a definite proposal of remedies for the abscesses in Denmark. The new beliefs under which H. D. wrote concerned themselves chiefly

106

with picayune Hellenic deities and demi-deities,
and anemic nature appreciations. Omitted tendencies included Vachel Lindsay's impressive
restoration of the tune and the chant to our
poetry; the ample extremist horde, captained
variously by Pound, Eliot, Kreymborg, Bodenheim, and others; the intense lyric of inner ex-
altation, as found in John Hall Wheelock, Edna
St. Vincent Millay, and elsewhere; the gentler
lyric, represented by Sara Teasdale, Margaret
Widdemer, and many more.

The opening study, upon Edwin Arlington
Robinson, suffers in comparison with one or two
later studies of the same poet; but it is friendly,
appreciative, and usually well considered. Robinson's background is sketched adequately, and
the volumes through *The Man against the Sky*
are interpreted with intelligence, if not acute
penetration. Faced with the next volume,
Merlin, Robinson's greatest achievement, Miss
Lowell's acumen deserts her wholly.

It is a long, meandering tale of some thirteen
hundred blank verse lines,

she says. It is some twenty-eight hundred lines
long. Her judgment is worse than her mathe-
matics: she can write,

He still remains the poet of the fleeting instant,

when her deserved extollation of *Isaac and Archibald, Ben Jonson Entertains a Man from Stratford,* and *Flammonde,* among his longer poems, wholly negatives the loose dictum; and when the briefest fragment of the poet's is the reverse of an interpretation of "the fleeting instant." Of the tremendous ending of *Merlin,* one of the high water marks of Robinson's magnificent poetry, she writes:

Merlin fails to satisfy because the ends ravel away without any such rounding.

Unfortunately for her critical reputation, this is the reverse of the case. Yet for her appreciation of the earlier Robinson she is entitled to praise.

Her treatment of Frost is much more superficial. Her comments are either tepidly obvious, or mistaken. Perhaps the fault at times is from her slovenly use of English, as when she paraphrases the theme of *Mending Wall* by saying that it indicates that walls are *built* (instead of mended) by two men working on opposite sides. Her misinterpretation of *The Fear* cannot be excused so readily. The poem ends with the panicky eloping wife, her fear reassured by

108

the full sight of the stranger near the dark farm-
house, fainting and falling to the ground. This
is told indirectly:

> She spoke as if she couldn't turn.
> The swinging lantern lengthened to the ground,
> It touched, it struck it, clattered and went out.

Miss Lowell's comment on this is the best criticism that can be made of her own critical
ability:

Does he kill her, or does she merely think that
he is going to do so? Which one is crazed, he
or she?

Neither is, of course, at all crazed. It is as if
her interpretation of *Jack and Jill's* ending were
a wonder whether he joined Christian Science,
or she did; and as to which of the two was a
mulatto. With an understanding as limited as
this, Miss Lowell's achievement as critic must be
likewise limited.

Characters and situations impress him, speech
does not.

This judgment is seriously warped away from
the fact. Frost's diction is his own speech, sen-
sitively reproduced: a speech moulded and keyed

to the speech around him. His magnificently colloquial rhythms are one of his crowns. When Miss Lowell comes to scan typical Frostian lines, she falls as emphatically by the wayside. All the Harvard pundits and all the claquing men can't set Miss Lowell on a pedestal again.

The chapter on Masters and Sandburg is uneven. She can say of Whitman's verse,

He found a free, almost rough, rhythmical prose the best instrument to his purpose.

Could a more unexpected flash of misunderstanding come from her, the polyrhythmic experimenter? Her appreciation of *Spoon River* is justified, although she overlooks its essentially superficial nature, limited to the unenlightened eyesight of the dead whose tongue is released by the soothing reaper; her dispraise of the author's succeeding books is as deserved. Sandburg is more difficult for her. She is "Amy Lowell, of Brookline, Massachusetts," to recur to M. Catel's description; and Sandburg, the radical, has qualities that could not fit into the Brookline universe. With prim seriousness she reprints nine bits from Sandburg's prose *Incidentals,* and answers each from her Brookline eminence. It must be confessed that the quotations she makes are mild repetitions of stock slogans widespread among liberals and radicals; but her answers are, if anything, more repetitive and hackneyed, and fail both in comprehension of his points and analysis of their worth. Her chief criticism of Sandburg's poetry—Ah, Miss Lowell, this sounds like your unintended confession of an understanding of your own chief lack—is "an occasional slip of grammar." Sandburg is so much more grammatical than the critic from Brookline that it is unfair to her to compare them. In general, she pays high earned tribute to his poetry.

Now comes the weak end of the book—the long concluding climactic chapter. The first two poets she pictured as overshadowed by the breakdown of old traditions; the second two, as swirling in the cynic and desperate chaos of an order during its delivery; and she has promised to give us two in conclusion, writing under "new beliefs," "living upon other planes of thought." These are the climax of the living American poets: above Robinson, Frost, Sandburg, Lindsay, Miss Millay, and all the rest—an implicit climax, poetically considered. These poets she selects as "H. D." and John Gould Fletcher.

Why did she pick these two Imagists, one an artificer of arty and pallid intaglios, the other a monument of cataracting verbosity, as America's best? There is but one answer: they were Imagists, and Miss Lowell was an Imagist. Ezra Pound was more logical than either of these, since he was a far better equipped poet: but his stature was taller than Miss Lowell's, and, besides, he had ceased calling himself an Imagist— as if that should have determined his ranking! A natural public modesty forbade her naming herself as the climax of our living singers; let us see what the two substituted starlings have to offer. She explains the choice of the Imagists as due to

the beliefs—moral, religious, and artistic—inherent in the characters of these poets.

Here we have the nadir of critical sense. Evaluating poets apart from their poetry, and from their moral, religious, and artistic beliefs, is as amazing an esthetic method as we have anywhere encountered. One might reasonably query what questionnaire was addressed to Robinson, Frost, Masters, Sandburg, Miss Millay,

AMY LOWELL

Lindsay, and the other American poets, demanding to know (1) their moral beliefs, (2) their religious beliefs, and (3) their artistic beliefs; and how the resultant answers were held to place them below the precious Imagist pair. Let us pass from this testimonial to their moral and religious beliefs (charitably assuming that Miss Lowell said this, without intending weight to be given to it), and behold the poetry they offer.

First of all, Miss Lowell restates the so-called Imagist credo, with elaborations. We give the simpler version:

1. To use the language of common speech, but to employ always the *exact* word.

2. To create new rhythms.

3. To allow absolute freedom in the choice of subject.

4. To present an image, (as opposed to the "cosmic" poet.)

5. To produce poetry that is hard and clear.

6. Finally, most of us believe that concentration is the very essence of poetry.

As she correctly proceeds, these principles are not new. They are overly dogmatic, of course. The first is an excellent principle, unless it be applied as a straitjacket. The second is a poetic virtue, albeit not an essential one. The third—let Miss Lowell give it its Brookline supplement—

within the bounds of good taste.

This is a timorous negation of the spirit of the principle. The fourth is obscure; even the cosmic poet presents images. The fifth may be accepted, until it hardens into dogma; the last was old when Poe insisted upon it.

A typical accoladed Imagist poem of H. D.'s is *Oread*:

> Whirl up, sea—
> Whirl your pointed pines,
> Splash your great pines
> On our rocks,
> Hurl your green over us,
> Cover us with your pools of fir.

The alert mind, as it cleaves through life, throws images to the side as a prow flings spray. Most of the images are as evanescent as the flung foam. There is a momentary resemblance between green waves and evergreen trees: yet, after all, waves are not pointed pines, nor pools of fir. The man who sees them once so is fortunate; the man who sees them twice so is forgiven. But the

114

man who sees them three times in this false guise is on the edge of seeing them always so: he may seek to hew a Yule tree from the foam, or bruise his diving head against the gnarled boles of the evergreen forest actuality. The image is a pretty fancy, and nothing more: the poem is a shaped dilution of nothing more. Among reasons for praising this poet, Miss Lowell states:

She seems quite unaffected by the world about her.

So are the dead. Miss Lowell points out that H. D.'s attitude is

to spend one's life longing for a vanished loveliness.

With sanity of vision the critic says:

This is a narrow art, it has no scope; it neither digs deeply nor spreads widely.

Among H. D.'s titles alone, we note *Acon, Hermes, Adonis, Pygmalion, Euridice, Hermonax, Sitalkas, Simaetha, Thetis, Leda, Hippolytus, Baia, Evadne, Phaedra, Hippolyta, Hymen, Heliodora, Lais, Nossis, Ion, Lethe,* and many more: "1. To use the language of common speech."

Turning to John Gould Fletcher, *The Vowels*, is praised among his poems:

A light and shade, E green, I blue, U purple and
    yellow, O red,
All over my soul and song your lambent varia-
    tions are spread.
A, flaming caravans of day advancing with
    stately art
Through pale, ashy deserts of grey to the shad-
    owy dark of the heart,
Barbaric clangor of cataracts, suave caresses of
    sails,
Caverned abysms of silence, assaults of infuriate
    gales;
Dappled vibrations of black and white that the
    bacchanal valleys track;
Candid and waxlike jasmine, amaranth sable
    black.

Lambent, clangor, abysms, infuriate (for in-
furiated), *bacchanal, amaranth:* "1. To use
the language of common speech." Of the two
poets, Miss Lowell's conclusion is:

Nature needed to be affirmed, and they affirmed it.

We only trust that nature is properly grateful.
There is much of Fletcher that is verbosely worse

than the example quoted; it is only in rare lines that he brushes beauty. John Quincy Adams, on his return to the House of Representatives after his incumbency of the presidency, was hailed for years as "Old Man Eloquent." It is in this tradition that Fletcher writes; not in the tradition of poetry, where "concentration is of the very essence," to return momently to the abandoned Imagist credo.

It is impossible to believe that Miss Lowell held that these were the two greatest living American poets. She placed them at the crown of the *Tendencies,* and then, with some penetration, mingled with her bin-bursting praise sharp knife-thrusts of keen criticism. It is difficult to read the unspoken mind of anyone: yet in this case many clues point the way. It is Imagism, after all, that she places at the pinnacle; and, in her own eyes and the eyes of the world, she, and not H. D. or Fletcher, represents Imagism. The book, then, appears in its real nature of an elaborate and sustained bit of sublimated log-rolling: a belligerent defense of her own right to be regarded as the chief poet writing in America. That her poetry does not establish her to this eminence we have already discovered: and the presence of this, as the underlying motive of the study, and the pilot of the author throughout, weighs against the book as impartial criticism. Impartial or not, it is recurrently inaccurate and obtuse.

In 1922 appeared *A Critical Fable*, published anonymously, whose authorship Miss Lowell soon admitted. Twenty-one poets are dealt with. Let us look first at the attitudes, and then at the expression. Much interest attaches to her opinion of her own work, as here expressed:

Conceive, if you can, an electrical storm
Of a swiftness and fury surpassing the norm;
Conceive that this cyclone has caught up the
    rainbow
And dashed dizzily on with it streaming in tow.
Imagine a sky all split open and scissored
By lightnings, and then you can picture this
    blizzard.
That is, if you'll also imagine the clashes
Of tropical thunder, the incessant crashes
Which shiver the hearing and leave it in ashes.
Remember, meanwhile, that the sky is prismatic
And outrageous with colour. The effect is
    erratic
And jarring to some, but to others ecstatic,

AMY LOWELL

Depending, of course, on the idiosyncratic
Response of beholders.

She is, she says, a swiftly furious electrical
storm, towing the rainbow after it; a blizzard
in a sky split by lightnings; tropical thunder,
and all outrageous with color.   This is not an
overdrawn picture of the glitter of her work.
It is a good criticism: and has not yet hinted
that the subject is a poet.   Some hail her with
ecstasy; she jars some,—true enough.

The lady's unique and surprising profusion
Creates in some minds an unhappy confu-
    sion. . . .
The future's her goose and I dare say she'll
    wing it,
Though the triumph will need her own power to
    sing it.

Sound again: "Unique and surprising profusion" is accurate; and, beneath the obvious
meaning, Miss Lowell has now come to realize
that, if she is to achieve worth as a poet, this
must come from future work, not from what
she has already done.   What has she done up to
this time?   Every volume of poetry published
during her lifetime: in spite of this, her hope is

that "the future's her goose." Death came; though, granted two score years more of life, there is small indication (except in *Nuit Blanche*) that she was improving.

> There's always a heart
> Hid away in her poems for the seeking; impas-
>   sioned,
> Beneath silver surfaces cunningly fashioned
> To baffle coarse pryings, it waits for the touch
> Of a man who takes surfaces only as such.

The average critical response would be that is not true of her: and the average critical response would be wrong. There is an impassioned heart hid away beneath the silvery surface; we will let it speak at length in the final chapter.

> Her books follow each other despite all the riot,
> For, oddly enough, there's a queer, crumpled
>   quiet
> Perpetually round her, a crazy-quilt tent
> Dividing her happily from the event.

Unfortunately this is true; we will note its significance later.

> A curious sight
> She makes in her progress, a modern White
>   Knight—

and we found in *Legends* the White Knight's song poorly parodied, though perhaps unconsciously, in *Many Swans*.

This is her picture of herself: mainly accurate, mainly self-understanding. In our final appraisal of her, let me repeat the astonishing fact that no attitude will be arrived at, which is not impressively stated of herself by Miss Lowell herself.

Frost, Robinson, and Sandburg are handled somewhat as in *Tendencies*; Masters gets rougher treatment:

They all have the stamp of back-alley lust. . . .
Mr. Masters, quite otherwise, thinks his creations
Reveal abstract truth in their vilest relations.
He sees every one as the suffering prey
Of some low, hidden instinct, his business to flay
The decency off them and show them all naked,
A few of them zanies, the rest downright
      wicked.

Lindsay is adequately praised; H. D. is caught off as "some ancient mirror"; Aiken is given as neurological and illogical:

He's so young as to think that he proves his ma-
      turity
By boldly colliding with all sorts of impurity,

—a judgment followed with praise of *Senlin's Morning Song* and *Punch*. Fletcher receives high homage, Sara Teasdale praise modified by—

She loves in a charming, perpetual way,
As though it just came when she was distrait,
Or quite occupied in affairs of the day.

Kreymborg is "the monkey of poetry who climbs on a stick," whose trade "consists largely in bluffing"; more than one of his efforts is said to be "a pimple on the fair face of poetry," although he too receives pianissimo praise. Eliot "has deserved his applause,"—such as it was, we add, with poetry (to let Miss Lowell continue)

The poems are expert even up to a vice,
But they're chilly and dead like corpses on ice.

We pass such vulgarisms as *like* for "as" here. Of Pound she says,

He's a belfry of excellent chimes run to jangle
By being too often and hurriedly tugged at,
And even, when more noise was wanted, just
    slugged at.

Benet receives hurried praise, Bodenheim is granted

Too little force and too much femineity.

AMY LOWELL

Why *femininity* was displaced for the awkward neologism is one of the countless mysteries of Miss Lowell's product. Edna Millay receives no mention, except a slighting one to *Aria de Capo* and the *Bean-Stalk,* there being a complete omission of her volumes *Renascence, Second April* and others, containing such magic as the title poem of the first, *God's World,* many exquisite sonnets, *The Blue Flag in the Bog,* the brilliant *Passer Mortuus Est,* the splendid *The Poet and His Book, Doubt No More that Oberon, Epitaph, Elegy, Travel, The Singing-Woman from the Wood's Edge,* and many more, the least of which is greater than any but two of Miss Lowell's poems, and the best of which is infinitely greater than Miss Lowell's best. It is no idle rumor that the Brookline critic was bitterly jealous of her woman rivals.

As for the manner of *A Critical Fable,* we have James Russell Lowell's *A Fable for Critics,* the kindred predecessor of this product, as a measuring stick. James Russell Lowell's verse was earth-bound; after seventy-four years, we may expect better verse from his niece. Lowell has many clever rhymes, such as:

treeified, deified; shoot us his, Brutuses; mistress, kiss trees; forest, no rest; dreamily, simile; here I see, conspiracy.

Three or four times he seeks to rhyme identities, which is a flaw, as identity is not rhyme. The examples noted are:

dialogue, die a log; portraits, poor traits; relieve, believe.

Among his few inept rhymes are—

visit, explicit; mistress, histories; have any, Daphne.

Amy Lowell has a number of clever rhymes, such as,

silence, mile hence; chimneys, trimness; bottle, hot Hell; better a, caetera; lackeys, back keys; course able, forcible; crams on, damson.

She has many identities instead of rhymes: in the first half, for instance,

motion, emotion; succeeded, preceded; exception, deception; tradition, erudition; deficiencies, efficiencies.

among others. Her off rhymes, or inept couplets of words which do not gracefully achieve rhyme or assonance, are multipliedly more than her predecessor's. The first type are of misplaced accent, as,

bombast, fast; pygmies, size; public, flick; prairies, seas; piano, so; rhetoric, stick; advantage, petulant age; recoil, turmoil.

The second type is mismatched consonants, as,

goddess, progress; absurdities, acerbities; pictures, mixtures; rainbow, in tow; desertion, diversion; genius, heinous.

A third type mismatches the number of syllables, as

centuries, entries; spirea, cafeteria; extras, dexterous; query, theory.

Such rhymes as *Euripides* and *snip idees, critics* and *sly ticks,* fail differently. Now the point to be noted is that light verse is a definite precinct of verse, with its master technicians, such as Carroll, Calverly, Lear, Gilbert, and many more in English literature, and with the two Carryls and Arthur Guiterman preeminent among Americans. The technique of the masters is, almost unexceptionally, flawless; the standard of light verse is extremely high. Since the aim is to amuse, delight, or pierce by satire, dexterity replaces pulsing appeals to the emotions in many instances; and dexterous the light verse must always be. Miss Lowell's *Fable* is not dexterous. Acceptable in the main as a restatement and broadening of her critical attitude on American poetry, her manner plumps down, in rhyme technique as well as the other ingredients of clever verse, almost as far as the Hudson Gorge. If it be offered in extenuation that the verses were meant to be casual and slipshod, we need not quarrel; they achieve that unimpressive aim.

Last of all we come to what Miss Lowell considered the major work of her life—her critical biography of John Keats, two thick volumes of more than eleven hundred pages of text. Here, if she was of full critical stature, her mature ability will be found. Her motive for undertaking the task, she announced in her preface, was to make public unrevealed facts about the English poet's life, which were available in her collection of Keatsiana, and in the collections of other Americans. Her intention

has been by no means to supplant existing biographies, but to add to them.

She would not have attempted a complete biography, she says, if it had been possible to present in any other way the facts she had discovered about Keats. This is well enough, as far as it goes; and yet, at first glimpse, it leaves much unexplained. At a similar first glimpse, the collocation of names—Amy Lowell, John Keats— seems incongruous to a high degree. We think of Keats, accurately or not, as a slim ethereal feminine type of poet, somewhat as we think of Shelley: with a face of unusual beauty, tending toward the feminine: and with a poetic flight, up from his few racked years, to the topmost heights of English song. We think of Amy Lowell as a massive, over-masculine woman, black cigars and all, a chip on both shoulders, fists squared, daring all comers to a constant fight: and, as a writer, spurting out cascades of fantastic modernistic word-glitter. Where is the tie, the connection, between gentle Keats and bellicose Miss Lowell? What was there in the life of Keats that could make her die for him— we quote Miss Sergeant again:

The two-volume Keats biography to which she almost literally gave her life, by allowing her working nights to impinge more and more seriously on her sleeping days over a period of years.

Why this intense devotion, to the flawless and exquisite technician, the helot to beauty whose snapped youth was buried under the overflowing violets near the pyramid of Caius Cestius? There have been a number of great English poets: why was it Keats, from the second poem in her first book onward, that held her utter allegiance? Why not rather belligerent Byron, waspish Pope, or the battered old fighter John Milton? What kinship of soul did she recognize, that laid upon her a compulsion (after her 1922 *Critical Fable,* with its confession of past failure worded "The future's her goose, and I dare say she'll wing it") to pour out her own racked life in this ample defense of England's Endymion?

The clue is found in what she recognized, consciously or subconsciously, as the essence of the Keatsian tragedy: that he, among great English poets, stood most tragically for unfulfilment in love. Among the other great singers, Chaucer, Spenser, Shakespeare, Milton, Burns, Coleridge, Wordsworth, Byron, Shelley, Browning, Tennyson, were satisfied variously in love: only Keats failed. In 1818, from his walking trip in Scotland, Keats wrote to his friend Bailey:

AMY LOWELL

After all I do think better of womankind than to suppose they care whether Mister John Keats five feet high likes them or not.

"Mister John Keats five feet high"—from the beginning, this had been his hideous irk. The ancestral background shrivelled to little, beside this. An 1816 sonnet began,

Had I a man's fair form;

in the presence of women, he wrote Bailey, his mind always insulted them grossly, and was "full of suspicions." Because of his height, no woman ever accepted him physically as her lover; what love he received he had to buy. He loved women, and fantasied them as his reciprocating loves; when they rejected him, this proved them false to his fantasy of them; hence the "suspicions." He wrote his sister-in-law of a casual woman that he met,

I should like her to ruin me, and I should like you to save me.

Endymion, of course a locked book to critics like Miss Lowell and Colvin, who lack the key of the new psychology, spreads this soul hurt of Keats to the sky, as I have elaborated elsewhere. To indicate briefly the substance of certain Keatsian paddings to the slim Greek myth of Endymion, the archetype of love in the poem is Cressid— Cressid, whom Keats omits to describe as the faithless. We recall the "suspicions." With titanic insistence he overturns all the old myths of chaste rejection, making Adonis yield to Venus, Arethusa to Alpheus, and Glaucus to the seductive Circe. In his fantasied world, since on earth "Mister John Keats five feet high" could not win any one woman that he desired, he has gods and near-gods alike yielding, wherever there is a love desire: and he has himself, as Endymion, "sleeping with Mistress Moon" throughout the whole long poem. All this was before he had met Fanny Brawne: and when he met her, the state of his morals and health prevented a physical mating; and so he went to his death unsatisfied.

Do we find this note anywhere in Miss Lowell's own poetry? In *A Fairy Tale,* in her first volume, she says that, overshadowing all the good gifts of her life,

is still the curse,
That never shall I be fulfilled by love!

In *Apples of Hesperides,* the line

> Yielding to no man's desire,

here torn bodily from its context, is not insignificant in our quest. In the next volume, writing of her heart "bleeding crimson seeds," she says,

> I, who am shut up, with broken crockery,
> In a dark closet!

The Max Breuck story is of wild love that turns out to be a drugged dream; Paul Jannes, in *The Shadow*, loved a shadow woman. In *Men, Women and Ghosts* the heart-wrung *Patterns* is a story of unfulfilled love; *The Cremona Violin* and *Reaping* give unsatisfied love as the motives for the infidelities. In the *Pictures*, one ends:

> Ah, Beloved, do you see those orange lilies?
> They knew my mother,
> But who belonging to me will they know
> When I am gone.

This is ended on a period, not an interrogation point. She was not asking a question. Such love must be heirless. *Snow in April* says,

> I am a plum-tree
> Checked at its flowering.
> My blossoms wither, . . .
> Dead,

With my blossoms brown and dropping
Upon my cold roots.

Appuldurcombe Park commences,

> I am a woman, sick for passion,
> Sitting under the golden beech-trees.
> I am a woman, sick for passion.

In *From a Yucca to a Passion Vine*, in *Legends*, the fox (a more aggressive American Endymion) assaults the moon. *The Statue in the Garden* tells of a man's love for a garden statue, made of lead. The posthumous volume contains, from a hokku:

> Love is a game—yes?
> I think it is a drowning.

There is a revealing poem cryptically entitled *Which, Being Interpreted, Is as May Be, or Otherwise*—almost a dare to the reader to arrive at its meaning. In it, Neron dreams consummation of love, but his dream is not strong enough, and his body is found,

> crushed beneath
> A fallen wooden statue, dead as nails.

In *The Green Parrakeet* she describes herself as

AMY LOWELL

> I may be
> A ghost myself, eternally
> Dreaming of the short, ironic bliss
> Of one long, unrepeated kiss.

In *The Red Knight,* she speaks with fantastic frankness, telling how she saw in a French church the vision of a knight in burning armor:

> I would have flung my kerchief to him to bind
>   upon his helmet,
> But kerchiefs fall obliquely through backward
>   centuries. . . .
> Steel footsteps on stone make a strange sound;
> I never heard the like before, and I think I never
>   shall again.
> For which unreasonable reason
> I am determined to remain a virgin.

In the *Critical Fable* she had said of herself,

> There's always a heart
> Hid away in her poems for the seeking; impas-
> sioned.

We have reached it sooner than we expected; we shall come to it again; and, throughout all her books, she says that it suffers from what she confessed in her first volume,

the curse
That never shall I be fulfilled by love!

This was one half of what she saw in Keats: incompletion in love.   Keats was (in appearance at least) over-feminine; Miss Lowell was, in appearance at least, over-masculine.   Incompletion in love was a persisting element in Miss Lowell's life, if her words mean what they say. There was another half of her picture of Keats —the world's chief picture of him, perhaps— his magnificent achievement in poetry, in spite of his failing health, his early death, his incompletion in love.   The fact of incompletion of love Miss Lowell apparently shared with the English poet: her desire, her wish-fulfilment, was to equal or come near his magnificent achievement in poetry.   This was a worthy desire in every way.   Thus she identified herself, consciously or subconsciously, with Keats, the incomplete in love, the magnificent poet.   The first half phrased her situation; the second, her desire.   Her self-draining tribute to Keats was, once the connection is understood, indirectly a tribute to the person whom she recognized as his modern counterpart,—herself.

This should throw some light upon her handling of the theme. The opening page is splendid prose, impassioned, filled with beauty. Never again does she reach such beauty for so long a stretch: but this indicates what she might have done in original prose. The telling is largely in her usual critical style, with copious quotations from original sources; and this gives high value to the book. It lacks completely the unity of aim, the coherence, the direct drive of such a study as Sidney Colvin's *John Keats*, a book contemporary with Miss Lowell's; and, of course, she lacks the Englishman's mellow style and sound erudition. In one matter of outlook, she is far more discerning than Colvin. He held that the passion for the "minx" Fanny Brawne hindered Keats's poetry; Miss Lowell, with far more insight, saw in the unsatisfied love for Fanny Brawne the very soul of the greatest of the poems of Keats. Her treatment on the whole, while undistinguished in detail, is ample, readable, and invaluable as a source book.

It is a pity that she could not bring to such a task a maturity of critical faculty, and some grace of phrase; for these might have made her book a masterpiece, instead of a necessary supplement to the encyclopedia account of the poet. Her treatment of Shelley, whom she calls "a plain, unadulterated crank," with a mind "all squeezed together into one little spot in an otherwise empty cranium," is the reverse of discerning. *The Masque of Anarchy* and other forthright Shelleyan words against the decaying scheme of things could not be forgiven by Brookline orthodoxy. She can leap in half a page from "I believe that this intimate experience with sorrow" to an acceptance of the belief as a truth, upon which she builds. She can write,

We regret "o'er" because it is a contraction which present-day poetry has agreed to drop,

as if the International Brotherhood of Poets and Versifiers had, by general referendum, acted upon the matter. The sentence unintentionally reveals that she is writing about herself, and not Keats: how could he have been subject to what "present-day poetry" was practicing? And, to pile Everest upon Pelion, Miss Lowell herself uses *o'er* in one word in her first book. She can write,

Keats was an almost completely modern man—

contemporaneous with herself, as she explains: this of Keats, who found in the golden past what his present denied him; Keats, building upon Spenser and the remoter English poets. But Miss Lowell saw herself as essentially a modern woman, or man: how could Keats fail to be one with her? What good would it do to list a score or more further instances of inadequate thinking, all in the first volume, or as many instances of misuse of the simplest rules of grammar and punctuation, as in these instances:

It had been printed a year earlier, in 1816, in a little paper-covered pamphlet, together with *Christabel* and the *Pains of Sleep,* so that Keats was already familiar with it, he may have owned it, certainly many of his friends did.

Or this:

Hood undoubtedly got his version from his wife, he had married Jane Reynolds.

That Miss Lowell entirely misses the point of *Endymion* was unavoidable, since she was unaware of modern analytic psychology. At least nothing in the first volume is quite as cobbling as this colloquialism from the second,

It was a pretty awful situation truly.

When it is pointed out that Miss Lowell held that
Meg Merrilies was

one of his very best poems. It stands unique in
his work,

her obtuseness to the subtleties of poetry becomes apparent. Again and again she is singu-
larly inept in her judgments, whether it be
inaccurately attacking the accuracy of her quotation from Keats's *Calidore*, or hailing high
beauty where high beauty is not. In dealing
with Keats, she had the great critical voices of
the past to steady her judgments; even at that,
she does not acquit herself more than passably.

It is impossible, then, to hail her *John Keats*
as a great essay in criticism, or to rank her, from
any or all of her critical writings, as an outstanding critic. She was a good fighter for her
own cause—good, if one forgives her wander-
ings from the best word usages. The random
prefaces and articles are unclear in thinking,
and full of errors of fact as well as grammar;
the study of French poets is pleasant, scattering,
graceless, and somewhat superficial; the study of
American tendencies is mere special pleading for
her own pet school of verse, built upon some

sound judgment of others; the light verse *Fable* is poorly done technically, and typical of her general attitude toward poetry; the biography of Keats, the topic chosen because this poet symbolized her inmost lack and longing, is invaluable for its copious quotations, and is a readable disintegrated treatment, marred by critical obtuseness and inexcusable slips from the standards of acceptable writing. In this secondary literary field she was a celebrity, rather than a distinguished interpreter.

V

THE IMPASSIONED HEART

We have found Amy Lowell acclaimed for her greatness as poet and critic by many voices; and, on examining her product, we have found her a celebrity in both fields, and neither a memorable poet nor a distinguished critic. If this study ended here, it would fail of the final function of criticism, which is interpretation. No matter how she sagged below greatness, the duty of the critic is to let her word speak, whatever that word was: to interpret her product to those she desired it to reach. That the real word she had to say will be surprising to many we may anticipate: it is rare that the substance of an art product floats like a pond-lily upon its surface. She herself described her heart as lying

Beneath silver surfaces cunningly fashioned
To baffle coarse pryings, it waits for the touch
Of a man who takes surfaces only as such.

140

Yet her desire, as phrased here, was that such a critic come, and reveal the real Amy Lowell beneath the veneer of Brookline attitude and printed glitter.

Greatness, in the widest sense, we have defined as that quality inhering in a product, by virtue of which it phrases the wish-fulfilments of the largest groups of people over a continuing stretch of time. If the wish-fulfilment satisfies a small group only, or even one individual, that would make the producer great, to the group or individual concerned; but it would withhold the general accolade forever. Let us see how closely Miss Lowell came to phrasing enduring and comprehensive wish-fulfilments. The wish-fulfilment may be apparently unique to the producer; but if it be shared by the world of men at large, he becomes their spokesmen. The love desire of Burns was his own uneasiness; but, since men and women thrill to the same unrest, he has become one of the laureates of love. In some such limited field we may find Miss Lowell expressing some general aspiration, which will qualify her to speak as the tongue of men, if not of angels. If she speaks in such a field with energy and sincerity enough, excessive flaws

141

of technique and music may be overlooked; though, if another speaks with the same energy and sincerity, added to an impeccable manner and tune, mankind would in the end rank the latter singer above the former.

Man's ultimate desires are few in number, and simple in character; of these, the instincts called hunger and love are preeminent in origin and force. Another powerful aspiration is the reach toward a god: as a symbolization of love unconsummated, as a dispenser of post mortem happiness denied before death, or as a satisfaction of some more misty desire. The first of these desires, hunger, could find no laureate in Miss Lowell. The hunger instinct is included by science among the preservative instincts, such as the wish for shelter, bodily covering, warmth, and the like. Miss Lowell had to conquer, says Miss Sergeant,

> riches, cushions, and conventions.

She was a coddled and pampered daughter of wealth from the start: man's spreading and desperate search after a livelihood for himself, his parents, his wife and children, never touched her immediately, and was never fully sensed by

142

her.   Bred in the stalwart Republican tradition,
she looked with inevitable non-comprehension,
at times twisted into a sneer, upon Shelley and
Sandburg alike: upon all spokesmen of the
under-dog's insistence that all canines were created equal in their rights to canine pleasures and
comforts.   She could never subscribe to the idea
that, if necessary, venerable artificial discrimi-
nations in rank, wealth, and opportunity must
be levelled to the wide dust: not that proletarian
injustice might follow, but that all men and
women might have an ampler chance to flower,
in the human garden, to their full stature.   This
preachment was no social and economic nihilism,
in essence, no wanton dynamiting of the past
and the cozy present enjoyed by the sheltered
affluent, but a broadening of the usefulness of
man's achievements, his ways of doing and
knowing things, until all might have their place
in the sun and the moony shadow that earth
holds imperturbably alike for all, before promot-
ing all to a more lasting and scattering seizin of
shadow.   The embracing ache of hunger was
sealed to her: she was closeted away from the
most desperate struggle that men have to face,
day after blank day.   This closeting relieved

her from the struggle for bread that has vul-
tured the bodies of so many poets. Her situation opened for her the frequent publication of
her overlong volumes, when better poets could
get no hearing. The bare publicity of ample
hearing, in its turn, holds its curse, as well as its
blessing. If their virtues were stifled, her faults
were blazoned by the same tilting of the scales.

This closeting did not bring her happiness,
which, after all, is much of the goal that wise
men see for man. She had her own gnawing
desires, and spoke them out for thirteen brilliant
years. These needs did not include a craving
after God. The first book contained a versified
stanza describing poetry, which was to

                              . . . make
Beauty a thing of awe; where sunbeams caught,
Transmuted fall in sheafs of rainbows fraught
With storied meaning for religion's sake.

Charity advises to refrain from quotation, since
so many faults emerge from their sepulture.
Sheafs, of course, is an improper plural, an error
for "sheaves." In spite of this fragment, there
is little religious craving in the first two books.
Instead, we have, among the *Sword Blades*, the

poem entitled *The Precinct. Rochester,* in
which she identifies herself as the Dean in the
Cathedral. She continues,

Beyond the Cathedral Close
Yelp and mutter the discontents of people not
    mellow,
Not well-regulated,
People who care more for bread than beauty,
Who would break the tombs of saints,
And give the painted windows of churches
To their children for toys.
People who say:
"They are dead, we live!
The world is for the living."

She has no sense of kinship with these: "Fools!
It is always the dead who breed," is her unsym-
pathetic comment. It still remains that people
without bread must care more for bread than
beauty; and daily they approach a widening
winning of this first goal, which is a gate
through which beauty may later be visited.
Nor is it the dead who breed physically: and
their spiritual breeding at times is death to the
living. Nor is the world rightly for the dead,
but for the living—the living in heart, the living in aspiration; the living in outlook, among

those whose blood is still quick. The curse was upon the Lady of Brookline: the windows of her vision were dark with the must of outworn centuries. Well-wishers to man can only trust that such windows may be washed clean with a flood not too red.

Ely Cathedral, in a later book, is mordant satire against the practice of religion:

Anæmic women, stupidly dressed and shod
In squeaky shoes, thump down the nave to laud
    an expurgated God. . . .
What is the red-flapped Bishop praying for, by
    the by?

The Swans, in the posthumous volume, repeats the theme of the Rochester poem, after eleven years. Miss Lowell is the Bishop this time; swarms of men, who do not care to hear "God's hours" beat, riot through the Cathedral, take the bells:

    We will melt them, and mold them,
    And make them a stem
    For a banner gorged with blood,
    For a blue-mouthed torch.

All the time the Bishop, "old, and kind, and deaf, and blind," potters along the moat-edge, admiring his swans. Subconsciously, at least, Miss Lowell saw herself, and her impotent futility in the fact of a soul-warped and demanding democracy.

In international affairs, she has poorly wrought stanzas against the practice of war, and a preoccupation with its glitter, coupled (as in the *Cornucopia of Comfits*) with a jingoist ability to whale down a Jonah of dishonest propaganda of Teutonic atrocities. To her credit let it be said that this verse, so far, has not appeared in any of her collected volumes. Her America she describes in *The Congressional Library*,

> without a race,
> Without a language,
> Of all races, and of none;
> Of all tongues, and one imposed;
> Of all traditions and all pasts,
> With no tradition and no past.

There is a smoke of truth here, though she overstates the case.

> But behind the vari-coloured hall?
> The entrails, the belly,
> The blood-run veins, the heart and viscera,
> What of these? . . .

There are words in the veins of this crea-
    ture, . . .
These are the voices of the furious dead who
    never die,
Furious with love and life, unquenchable, . . .
This is the music of the Trumpeters of the Al-
    mighty
Weeping for a lost estate,
Sounding to a new birth which is to-morrow.

This is ambiguous, and intuitively a step toward
truth. There is no religious implication, in
spite of "Almighty"; she seems to point to poets,
then to the great demanders of man's lost estate,
which would mean the world's radical voices.
She hardly accepted this consciously; and, of
course, the "entrails, the belly, . . . the heart
and viscera" of our land are the silenced hosts
of labor, in farm and manufacturing plant, although she could not see this.

Thus we find her spokesman neither for the
hunger forces, nor the desire for God; we find
her undistinguished as a singer of pacifism and
patriotism alike; we find her aligned against in-
surgent democracy. There remains the most
powerful inner imperative, the love force: and
her reference to her hidden "impassioned heart"

indicates that she has her word to say upon this. What is this word?

Her first book, and the other quotations given in the discussion of the Keats volume, indicated the abiding nature of one aspect of her problem: that of an unsatisfied longing for love—

> the curse
> That never shall I be fulfilled by love!

The desire for fulfilment, if not the curse of un-fulfilment, is a general human characteristic. But there are certain outside elements in this poet's case, which indicate that her attitude may not coincide with the human norm. Her masculine appearance, her "big black cigars," her masculine belligerency, her "fleshly discom-fort," to quote Miss Sergeant's charitable phrase, may account for the actual curse of non-fulfilment. Let us look more closely at the am-ple chronicles of love in her volumes. The first described her as "a careless boy," "a little boy," a boy playing with the angel boy who had the Pleiades as toys; it referred to her boyish games, with small mention of girlish games. From childhood, apparently, she regarded herself as a boy, if her verse accurately describes this detail.

149

Since the choice was free with her to use either description, and the other would be the more expected and grooved in the normal, the alteration is significant. It is in such apparently unimportant details, let it be remembered, that the artistic producer is most revealing. In two poems, *Crowned* and *The Promise of the Morning Star*, she takes the woman's attitude; in nine, she regards herself as a man. The first calls herself, as poet,

> The shredded remnant of a man.

In *Hora Stellatrix* she is a passionate male wooer:

> So give: ripe fruit must shrivel or fall.
> As you are mine, Sweetheart, give all!

Her amorous desire was, at least, not humble. In *Dipsa* she asks the garden

> To sanctify and bless our night of love . . .
> For you have given all yourself to me
> Making me gentle by your willingness.

The adultery motif appears gently in *The Road to Avignon*; it will become one of her dominant narrative themes, somewhat as if, denied licit fulfilment, her desire broadened to include a desire for the illicit as well.

AMY LOWELL

The autobiographical love tone appears in *Venetian Glass:*

> For you I have shed bitter tears, for you
> I have relinquished that for which my heart
> Cries out in selfish longing.   And tonight,
> Having just left you, I can say: " 'Tis well."

A Little Song begins,

> When you, my Dear, are away, away,

and prays that, after the return, the moon may

> Watch over a century of nights.

This is not a bad beginning, for the first book.

In two poems in the second book, it is unclear whether the lover is a man or woman speaking. Five poems picture the poet as a woman; one, as a boy; some twenty, as a man. *A Gift,* commencing

> See! I give myself to you, Beloved!

sounds like the woman's attitude; one of the others so grouped is a narrative of a woman who had been betrayed. As man, she pictures herself as the Dean of Rochester, frequently as poet, and repeatedly as lover. The scent of a woman's blue scarf "lingers and drugs me"; the poet longs for the loved woman:

And I wished for night and you.
I wanted to see you in the swimming-pool,
White and shining in the silver-flecked
    water. . . .
Night, and the water, and you in your white-
    ness, bathing!

This is the man's attitude, though the poet may
be speaking as a woman with the man's attitude.
Aubade suggests a kindred idea:

As I would free the white almost from the green
    husk
So would I strip your trappings off,
Beloved.
And fingering the smooth and polished kernel
I should see that in my hands glittered a gem be-
    yond counting.

It is possible to read such a poem abstractly:
but both elements are intrinsically in the poem.
As suggested, "man's attitude" may mean only
the imperative love insistence ordinarily typical
of man; or it may mean actual identification of
the poet as a man.   In the opening poem, where
she as poet is pictured definitely as a man, she
says of herself:

      The tearless sobs tore at my heart.

On one memorable platform occasion in Philadelphia, she wept similarly; and there are other instances. The adultery theme is emphasized twice in the book.

Men, Women and Ghosts consists largely of stories; the theme at least thrice is adultery, with seduction occurring at least once. *Patterns,* the excellent opening-poem, emphasizes unfulfilled love, fantasied in a medieval setting. *Can Grande's Castle* is made up of four long examples of polyphonic prose, in which the symbolism is more hidden than in the briefer lyrics. *Pictures of the Floating World,* however, swings us back to the more intimate love songs. Perhaps six of the poems take the woman's attitude; three times as many take the man's. There is an additional group of some score of poems in which the attitude is masculine, although it is indicated clearly that the poet is speaking in her own person. The only noteworthy poem among the number where the poet clearly speaks as woman is *Appuldurcombe Park,* already referred to, with its opening:

I am a woman, sick for passion.

Those taking the man's attitude are at times vague, at times very distinct:

I followed a procession of singing girls
Who danced to the glitter of tambourines,
Where the street turned at a lighted corner,
I caught the purple dress of one of the dancers,
But, as I grasped it, it tore,
And the purple dye ran from it
Like blood
Upon the ground.

This is one of her *Dreams in War Time*. Most interesting of all is the group called *Two Speak Together*, a volume of love poems, at times impassioned, from the poet to another woman. The opening one asks,

Why are you not here to overpower me with
　　your tense and urgent love?

The second confesses,

I am tired, Beloved, of chafing my heart against
The want of you; . . .
And I scald alone, here, under the fire
Of the great moon.

After describing the beloved, she speaks more directly:

　　　Was Venus more beautiful
　　　Than you are,
　　　When she topped
　　　The crinkled wave?

154

AMY LOWELL

She refers to

> The words I blew about you
> To cover you to great loveliness
> As with a gauze
> Of misted silver.

In *Madonna of the Evening Flowers,* the poet-lover says to the beloved woman,

> And I long to kneel instantly at your feet.

The whole thing—beloved lady and all—for all its factual reality, has some element of unreality about it: as if the love is at core a nothingness. It is described as

> As solid as the center of a ring of fine gold.

The beloved woman leans against the poet, as they watch the fireflies; and then—

> You stand between the cedars and the green
>   spruces,
> Brilliantly naked. . . .
> And I see you are fire,
> Sacrificial fire on a jade altar.
> Spear-tongue of white, ceremonial fire.
> My eyes burn,
> My hands are flames seeking you,

although in this unbared poem the beloved lady continues remote.   *Interlude* ends,

The moon,
Still,
Upon your face.
You shine, Beloved,
You and the moon.
But which is the reflection? . . .
I think, when we have shut and barred the door,
The night will be dark
Outside.

There is more than the mere concetti in this conclusion.   Again we have the lady adjured to hide
her face,

> For I am blinded by your beauty,
> And my heart is strained,
> And aches,
> Before you.
> In the street
> You spread a brightness where you walk,
> And I see your lifting skirts
> And rejoice;

but when the poet-lover looks at the lady's face,
her strength is melted, her knees "set to trembling."   Again, in *Summer Rain,*

> All night our room was outer-walled with
>   rain. . . .
> But to me the darkness was red-gold and crocus-
>   coloured

156

With your brightness,
And the words you whispered to me

flamed like orange torches against the rain.   In
Opal,

You are ice and fire,
The touch of you burns my hands like
    snow. . . .
When I am with you,
My heart is a frozen pond
Gleaming with agitated torches.

Wakefulness, in the dark,

And still you sleep!
Tired heart of my joy, . . .
Will the day come before you have opened
    to me?

In the midsummer she writes,

   You beckoned me over a rainbow bridge,
   And I set foot upon it, trembling.

The beloved woman holds out a cup to the poet-
lover:

But the water in the cup was scarlet and crim-
    son
Like the poppies in your hands.

"It looks like blood," I said.
"Like blood," you said,
"Does it?
But drink it, my Beloved."

In these poems the symbolism wears very thin. *Nerves* has the beloved one dead and buried; but immediately thereafter she is resurrected again. This tells us that the death and burial, as we might have expected, was a mere wish-fulfilment. That element at the gate of consciousness called the censor, which warps the subconscious fantasies into something acceptable to the consciousness, is evidently at work: the "agen-bite of in-wit," located in the censor, wishes the beloved dead, as one solution of the unrest. To show the workings of the censor, if the subconscious wish were that of a sadist, who desired to shed blood, the censor might twist this into an accidental shedding of blood, accompanied by grief on the part of the shedder; or might transform it into a spilling of grape juice, as a symbol thinly hidden. In *Nerves*, if we read it correctly, the former method is used: the poet-lover directly dreams death for the Beloved, emotionalizing it with a thin regret, to make it acceptable to the consciousness.

AMY LOWELL

In *Autumn,* the poet-lover, speaking of a dahlia, asks:

> Shall I send it to you,
> You who have taken with you
> All I once possessed?

Strain has the poet-lover

Stretching out my arms to comfort myself with
    you,
Clasp instead the cold body of the darkness,

described with a fulness of detail,

> All night it will hunger over me,
> And push and undulate against me
> Breathing into my mouth.

This is the reverse of an ignorance of love-practices. *Haunted* is an equally fantastic case of shadowy mating; *Grotesque* has a displeasing sadistic element. *Preparation* is a brilliant bit of love evocation, where the poet-lover buys smoked glasses, to avoid being blinded by the sight of the beloved woman after absence. *A Decade,* in its epigrammatic completeness, tells how the beloved woman, at first, was like "red wine and honey," which burnt the mouth with sweetness:

Now you are like morning bread,
Smooth and pleasant.
I hardly taste you at all for I know your savour,
But I am completely nourished.

Again the symbolic veneer cracks a trifle.
After her death, the poet-lover says, her love will
continue to speak to the beloved woman through
the accustomed furnishings of the room,

As it does now through my voice,
And the quick necessary touch of my hand.

The last poem in the series has the same love
note, and a definite statement that the poet-
lover will die first. This need not be taken as
prophecy, in the sense of a foreglimpse of something fated; it is rather prophecy, in the sense of
something willed by the poet-lover herself: the
thing, indeed, which came to pass. One of the
things men are learning slowly is that death itself is a slave to the strong ones of life: that, if
they cannot name its hour of coming, they can
at least approximate this. This decision need
not be conscious, nor need it be without unconscious conflict; but if the weight of the tendencies leans toward a welcome to death, death does
not long delay. Two men start to cross a

traffic-perilous street. The one who is integrated in his desire for life is warned, by every conscious sense and every half-conjectural unconscious tentacle, of each danger, and crosses in safety. The one whose underlying tendency is toward death receives the warnings obtusely or erroneously, receives false unconscious monitions, and steps "unintentionally" in the face of the slashing motor that spells death. This is an extreme case; in subtler ways the hidden tendency operates, speaking cryptically or clearly (as here) its word, and then in hidden ways bringing it to pass. We have graduated from the elementary attitude of "Seeing that death, a necessary end, will come when it will come." In this poem the poet-lover, picturing herself as a red aster and the beloved woman as a purple one—she had queried of the beloved,

Why do you subdue yourself in golds and purples?

in a previous poem—in speaking of death, says:

    You or I—and I am a coward.
    Surely frost should take the crimson.
    Purple is a finer colour,
    Very splendid in isolation.

So we nod above the broken
Stems of flowers almost rotted.
Many mornings there cannot be now
For us both.   Ah, Dear, I love you!

It is impossible to feel anything but an abiding pity for this self-vision of cold roots tighten-
ing, and a general wreckage of life, which could
induce this love cry out of an old desperation,
joined with a sense of the brief years remaining,
and of the poet's death before that of her closest
woman friend.   For the years were brief: and
the poet has died.

During the six years remaining, *Legends* appeared.   Its opening poem, a strange reversal of
the Endymion motif that self-symbolized Keats,
has the poet as the "small red fox" that

Weeps in little yelping barks for the cold beauti-
    ful body
Of the inaccessible moon.

When the moon appears, the fox wins its fantastic desire,

With staring eyes
And ghoulish, licking tongue.
Satyr fox assailing the moon! . . .
Upon the disk of the moon are spots, black ob-
    scene spots, the print of a fox's paws.

AMY LOWELL

Many Swans, Indian hero of the poem named after him, secures the bright sun to hang around his neck; and with it burns to death all people, including all whom he loves. There was a bright glitter in this poet's work, and she may have seen it as a blight to love. In *Witch-Woman*, the poet is the lover of the witch, with her

> Thighs and breasts I have loved,
> Lips virgin to my thought,
> Sweeter to me than red figs. . . .
> Death is cool and kind compared to this,
> This horror which bleeds and kindles,
> These kisses shot with poison,
> These thoughts cutting me like red knives.

This love, these thoughts, echo that "agen-bite of in-wit" that we found before. The lover promises his god to love the woman suspected of being a witch, as a test of her nature. She rises and stands in the moonlight like an obelisk:

> Naked and white, the matron moon urges the
> woman. . . .
> She is naked before the naked moon.

The symbolism clarifies. The witch-woman's goat-skin clothing leaves, her flesh goes too; she is "a skeleton dancing in the moon-green air" "in a crepitation of lust," and mounts to blend with the moon, which alters swiftly to a crimson rose, a black-tongued lily, "a purple orchid with dark, writhing bars." The purple orchid echoes something we have heard before. In the end, the lover plunges his sword into his own heart, and offers to his god the flesh cast from the witch-woman's black soul. Some may prefer to take the poem as a purely objective study; but the dénouement of witch-woman loving moon-woman, the latter altering to a purple orchid, gives it weight as supplement to the love songs already considered.

Concerning *The Ring and the Castle*, a study of adultery and sadistic murder of the errant wife by the lover, Miss Lowell says, in her preface, that its inspiration is lost irrevocably. Of course, this points to an activity of the censor. Jean Catel writes of the poem that when

she (Miss Lowell) heard, one morning, a sentence ringing in her mind: "Benjamin Bailey, Benjamin Bailey, why did you get up at the stroke of three?" she mistook it for poetry. And she thought there lay the germ of a poem. She then wrote one of her *Legends*.

164

AMY LOWELL

Benjamin Bailey, by the way, was a friend of Keats, who is referred to more than fifty times in Miss Lowell's biography of the English poet. Evidently she received the name from this source, and needed no other inspiration but the inner compulsion to phrase another study of the adultery theme, complicated with sadism. *Gavotte in D Minor* is a picture of a woman "chill and uncosseted (unfondled)" like the moon:

> She jeers at life, must she wed instead
> The cold dead?

And she dies,

> And they wept her virgin soul.

The personal implication again is overwhelming. In *The Statue in the Garden,* the poet identifies herself with the man who loves a garden statue made out of lead:

> Now 'twas but sex
> Deprived its due reason,

which caused the man's condition, she says: and the use of "reason" here is odd, and faintly revelatory. After a brilliant paraphrase of Robinson (the nine lines commencing "And I'm not saying that there were no moments") comes a love episode:

Her beautiful, beautiful mouth, her sucking, in-
    tolerable mouth—

strange adjectives to apply to a lead statue! A lead Gardener is purchased as mate for the statue, to liberate the human lover; and in a mad phantasmagoria of murder she appears,

                The strands
Of her shredded petticoat dabbed with blood,
She follows Julius, the Gardener behind
Runs with a frothy, scarlet cud
Oozing out of his mouth—

a riot of fantastic adultery and dreadful sadistic murder. A seer once wrote,

It will have blood, they say; blood will have
    blood.
Stones have been known to move and trees to
    speak;
Augurs and understood relations have
By magot-pies and choughs and rooks brought
    forth
The secret'st man of blood.

Poetry, as well, will in the end speak as well as
  166

AMY LOWELL

move, discovering the frothy scarlet cud and the
impassioned heart as well.

The posthumous *What's O'Clock* has the poet
as woman only twice, once in the revealing *The
Red Knight*, already referred to, where a vision
of a medieval knight replaces a human lover in
her mind,

> For which unreasonable reason
> I am determined to remain a virgin.

More often she appears as the man, or as the aggressive lover with masculine characteristics.
Evelyn Ray is a story of love's unfulfilment.
She rivets the identification of herself as Many
Swans by the poem, *The Swans*, in which she is
the Bishop, as she was the Dean of Rochester
long before—this time an aged ecclesiastic, "old,
and kind, and dead, and blind"—no half-lidded
vision of the result of the Brookline tradition.
We learn soon—

> The lady of my choice is bright . . .
> As a purple-hearted clematis.

We have had the purple aster, the purple orchid,
and in the same volume:

167

AMY LOWELL

A queen pacing slowly through the Parthenon,
Her dress a stare of purple.

Vespers has misty implications, *In Excelsis* speaks
more clearly:

I drink your lips,
I eat the whiteness of your hands and feet.
My mouth is open,
As a new jar I am empty and open.
Like white water are you who fill the cup of my
        mouth. . . .
I dare reach to you,
I dare touch the rim of your brightness. . . .
My throat sings the joy of my eyes,
The rushing gladness of my love. . . .
I do not thank you,
I take you,
And live.

White Currants ends

        So long as you accept them
        And me.

The subconscious often engenders strange puns.
The *On-Looker* is hardly more than ambiguous,

Such to a woman stretched upon a bed of battle,
Who bargained for this only in the whispering
        arras
Enclosed about a night of enchantment.

168

AMY LOWELL

Which, Being Interpreted, Is as May Be, or Otherwise, with its audaciously taunting title, daring the reader to solve its riddle, tells the story of old Neron, who discovers the statues of a king and a lovely queen.

> She stood as naked to old Neron's eyes
> As though no robe were there.

Neron creates a dream life of the king, the queen, and himself,

> . . . A proper youth whose sap ran hot
> Over his gusty body, ripe for love,
> Fresh with the burning agony of love.

The king enters upon his liaison with the queen:

> But the dream halted at this very spot,
> He could not push it to a consummation.

The queen yields in desire, the tryst commences, the king bursts in, and measures the might of his dream against Neron's. The verger

> . . . Came at last upon him, crushed beneath
> A fallen wooden statue, dead as nails.

It is not hard to see Neron as the poet, old, and, in fantasy, "a youth . . . fresh with the burning agony of love"; and to read the desire for

the woman-queen, and the struggle with the
world-king (environment, body, and all) which
killed the dreamer in the end. "Or Otherwise,"
as you choose.

The Sisters has the poet addressing Sappho,

Ah, me! I wish I could have talked to Sappho,
Surprised her reticences by flinging mine
Into the wind.

Sappho was not noted for reticences, by the way.

This tossing off of garments
Which cloud the soul is none too easy doing
With us today. . . . We two were sisters
Of a strange, isolated little family.

Superficially the family referred to is that of
woman poets. Her summary (referring, be it
noted, to love, not poetry) is—

Which way shall I go?
Sappho spent and gained; and Mrs. Browning,
After a miser girlhood, cut the strings
Which tied her money-bags and let them run;
But Emily hoarded—hoarded—only giving
Herself to cold white paper. Starved and tor-
tured,
She cheated her despair with games of patience,
And fooled herself by winning.

170

AMY LOWELL

Emily is Emily Dickinson, and "patience" is the game of cards more commonly called solitaire. On the surface Miss Lowell is describing the love solutions of the three, be it remembered. Emily—

Hung her womanhood upon a bough,
And played ball with the stars—too long—too
    long.

Miss Lowell ends,

I understand you all, for in myself—
Is that presumption?   Yet indeed it's true—
We are one family.   And still my answer
Will not be any one of yours, I see.

This is forthright talking: in herself she embodies the love attitudes and desires of Sappho, Elizabeth Barrett Browning, and Emily Dickinson with her patience.   Amy Lowell's answer will not be "any one of yours," she says.   What fourth possibility is there, unless it lies to left or right of Emily Dickinson, or is a blend of two or three of the methods?

   Fool o' the Moon brings in the moon woman, as constantly,

With a single breast uncovered,
The carnation tip of it

Urgent for a lover's lip . . .
I stand watching, waiting, gazing,
All of me spent in amazing,
Longing for her wheat-white thighs. . . .
And a goodly company
Of men are we,
Lovers she has chosen. . . .
Hush, then, let me say it soon,
I have lain with Mistress Moon.

The tendency in the whole of the love poetry points overpoweringly to the conclusion that her attitude lies between that of Sappho and that of a masculine lover. *The Green Parrakeet* has the poet:

Then I knocked at the door and entered in
Like the orange flame of a hidden sin.

The wording is not insignificant.

I tossed her arms apart and pressed
Myself upon her, breast to breast, . . .
I forced her lips till they caught on mine,
And poured myself down her throat like wine.
I mingled with her, part for part.

Yet in the end she may be

A ghost myself, eternally
Dreaming the short, ironic bliss
Of one long, unrepeated kiss.

Contemplating the last two passages, there remains no doubt as to her love desire, which is worded almost invariably as a wish fulfilled. Her calling herself a man in this poem is negatived by the concluding summary and interpretation of the earlier love passion. A love-song misnamed *A Grave Song* contains,

I've a pocketful of emptiness for you, my
    Dear . . .
Can you flourish on nothing and find it
    good? . . .
If you can, I will go and lay me down
And kiss the edge of your purple gown.
I will rise and walk with the sun on my head—

The touch of purple is familiar; and the mention of sun supplements the identification of the poet as Many Swans.

The poet qualifies surely as an impassioned singer of her own desires; and she may well be laureate also of as many as stand beside her. Modern psychology suggests the hypothesis that this number is increasing. There was such a blend, of the characteristics of the two sexes, in Shakespeare (as witness his sonnets), in Shelley, in Byron, in Whitman; yet these remained predominantly men, with a man's attitude; and in their poetry these poets phrase as a rule normal human love in quality, however excessive the quantity may be. Miss Lowell was not predominantly the woman in attitude; she was almost the reverse. Yet she was a woman; which brings up the essential paradox of her being and singing, the essential limitation of the group for whom she speaks. What causes achieved this result are matters for scientific research, in hers and other cases; the fact is spread publicly throughout her books. It leaves her a singer of her own type of love, rather than a tongue for the great desire whose sublimation is civilization.

In this study, now nearing its end, we have throughout based our conclusions upon Miss Lowell's own words; and it will be of value to see what, from the first, was her picture of herself. The first poem in the first volume pictures her as

> Seeds withered unsown, . . .
> The shredded remnant of a man.

Her life's philosophy may be summed up, insurgency and all, in her line:

The law exacts obedience. Instruct, I will conform.

174

Progress is the fruit of the non-conformers. She conformed to the law peculiar to her own nature. She says,

> So I behold my visions on the ground
> No longer radiant, an ignoble heap
> Of broken, dusty glass.

This volume refers to her "fading youth," whose longing is "to be some other person for a day"; in the next, she calls her voice an "oblation from a shattered urn." Of the wine in her "goblets of desire" she says:

Spilt is that liquor, my too hasty hand
Threw down the cup, and did not understand.

She suffers pain, and "may not endure till time can bring (her) ease."

> Happiness: We rarely feel it.
> I would buy it, beg it, steal it,
> Pay in coins of dripping blood
> For this one transcendent good.

She is a good fighter:

I have not quailed,
I was all unmailed,
And naked I strove, 'tis my only vaunt.

The *Tale of Starvation* has personal implications. Again,

Have at you, you Devils!
My back's to this tree. . . .
Come on now, all three! . . .

Yet she says,

So I do, but my heart
Is the heart of a man.

Of what use is her sword-like brain, she asks,

I, who am set to crack stones
In a country lane!

This is an astonishing picture of her conception
of her affluent Brookline situation. When she
desires red berries,

But, in the mist, I only scratch my hand on the
thorns.
Probably, too, they (the berries) are bitter.

She can see all around her, she says in *Pictures,*

only sand,
Sand lying dead in the sun,
Lines and lines of sand,
Sand.

She is the trained dancing bear, with cobbles
cutting her feet. In *After Writing "The Bronze
Horses"* she says:

176

AMY LOWELL

I am so tired.
I have run across the ages with spiritless
   feet. . . .
I have written things
Which sucked the breath
Out of my lungs, and hung
My heart up in a frozen death.

This ends in terrible despair:

A body peeled
Down to a skeleton,
A grinning jaw-bone in a bed of mignonette.
What good is it to say "Not yet."
I tell you I am tired
And afraid.

Last of all, her posthumous volume intensifies
the wither of disillusionment. *Footing up a
Total* contrasts her achievement with that of a
"highly unsuccessful confrère," with her start:

I move to the sound of gold, and brass, and
   heavily-clashed silver. . . .
Alas! and when they have clanged me to my
   grave . . .
What then, my friend?

Will one who comes from her funeral
. . . remember bones and shouting do you
   think? . . .

Your health, my highly unsuccessful confrère,
Rocking your seed-bells while I drift to ashes.
The future is the future, therefore—
Damn you!

A typical masculine ending; and she sees accurately that all that will survive her is "bones and shouting." *La Ronde Du Diable* tells, in harsher words than I could use, what she was as critic:

That's a tune we all dance to.
Little poet people snatching ivy,
Trying to prevent one another from snatching
    ivy.

This is witheringly true of her: instead of being encouraging and helpful to others, she (as she damned the unsuccessful confrère) spent her life snatching toward ivy she could not reach, and trying to prevent the other poets from taking the ivy they were entitled to.

I want your leaf, Brother, and you mine. . . .
"Here we go round the laurel-tree."
Do we want laurels for ourselves most,
Or most that no one else shall have any?

This was Amy Lowell as critic—the second alternative, as she implies. She calls her art

AMY LOWELL

> A little gift of speech
> Set a cubit higher than the common reach.

She was an optimist about her worth, rather than a pessimist. Bones and a shouting, as person and poet; snatching at ivy and laurel, and trying to prevent other poets from having any laurels, as critic,—so she saw herself, with terrible clarity. My early review of her *Tendencies* stated that the book was sublimated log-rolling; and, as has been stated, she wept at her inability to convince me that the opposite was so. But time has come round, in *What's O'Clock;* and with ultimate honesty she has stated, concerning her critical work, far worse than my dictum.

Her uneven tribute to Keats we have found based upon her identification of herself with the English poet; her extollation of H. D. and Fletcher, broken with sharp stabs of discerning depreciation, was in its tribute aimed at herself, as the Imagist leader, rather than at her less prominent followers. Yet, after all, she saw more in some of her contemporaries (except in Miss Millay and other rival women poets) than this ivy-snatching and laurel-snatching passage would lead us to believe. She was a fairer critic than her own words admit. Her abiding obtuseness to subtleties of beauty was innate and irremediable. Her abiding faults of utterance must lie in the scanty education furnished by the private schools which she attended. The two alternatives are that these exclusive schools taught her adequately, and that she forgot the rudiments of grammar and rhetoric; or that the schools failed to base her scrappy erudition upon a secure groundwork. The latter of these two is the more probable. As poet, she described herself as a mere "shouting." This again is more unkind to her than her product displays. As a craftsman she lacked ultimate finality of utterance, the creative ability to bring up from her subconsciousness word music so overpowering emotionally that it earns inclusion in the few high strains which the heart of man remembers. She could not hear this music, or say it, or recognize it in others, judging by her varied product. This can be only the opinion of one critic, uttered honestly as a hypothesis toward guiding the judgment of the future; and the future may overturn the dictum wholly. I should be glad to see the opinion reversed, for Miss Lowell's sake, if her work earns it. But, in spite of this negative opinion as to her supreme excellence, much remains that is more than a "shouting." *Patterns* is a flawed masterpiece, *Nuit Blanche* is more. There is a great heave of colorful brilliance in much of the polyphonic prose, unpoetic though the medium may be. There are many slighter verses and parts of poems that earn at least an immediate deathlessness.

Her critical attitude, as revealed in the laurel-snatching poem, is hopeless: and she aims it as an indictment against all her contemporaries. If this were the general attitude of American poets, the outlook would lower depressingly. My whole impression is that she speaks for herself and some of her intimates and contemporaries, but by no means for the finer few of them. Not one of the leading half dozen poets in America, as far as I have ever noted from printed or spoken word, had this attitude. Many of the leaders are notably unselfish in their attitude toward the lesser poets around them. They can afford to be: Miss Lowell could not. Or shall I rather say that they are selfish, in the sense that they see that no petty line of ego ownership divides their work one from the others; but that all are alike tongues for their age, and that the cause of each is aided, and not retarded, by excellence among the others? This enlightened and widened selfishness is, luckily for us, far commoner than Miss Lowell said or saw. Dispraise of herself she saw as personal prejudice, since (her own poem confesses it absolutely) her own dispraise of others was personal prejudice. Dispraise of her work was at times required by a sincere fidelity to the cause of poetry, that she and the other poets alike served. She could not see this: she was as she was.

In her egotistic belligerence, she was not accustomed to underrating her own worth. Yet we have found her, in a relaxed mood of sincerity, sagging below accuracy in self-depreciation. Her poetry was more than a mere "shouting"; her criticism at times rose above mere log-rolling. Most of all, her influence was a potent force in the whole modern trend. Not a beneficial force always as a rule, in all probability. With her whole armory of axes to be sharpened, and equipped with the material welfare that armed her for many subtle compliments of board and shelter, she pushed somewhat ruthlessly toward her conception of poetry: which

182

was something alien to what clear vision would have given her. Yet she was aligned with the experimenters, rather than the technical conservatives; and art needs the experimenters. Perhaps her polyphonic prose will endure as an art from suburban to prose and poetry, with city conveniences and country advantages; perhaps it will die the death of the excrescential sport. Living or dead, it has contributed something to the poetic era. Her astonishing range of topics (for all that she chose and used them to word her own situation and longings), a range extending from the ancient Inca to the latest jazz, from the hour of plumed knights, of Napoleon, of Nelson, of Perry, to the arrogantly questioning present, has in itself a liberating force, in awaking the poets to the amplitude of their possible field. She saw herself from the start as a failure in life, due to physical facts that made her "unfulfilled in love"; and this attitude mired and spotted her whole conception of life. In spite of this, she fought well and gallantly, with all of the immense vigor that sublimated out of frustration, for what was near to her heart. She popularized modern poetry— or her preferences in it—to much of a continent, in the eyes of parts of America incarnating the starburst in herself. She was a person, a celebrity; and many a more gifted person has remained, to the world, persistently less, low though her absolute achievement may be.

There can be no attitude but that of pity for the irks which plagued her; yet with this will go the realization that, but for these irks, she might have been a silence where she is—or was —a sound of many walls falling. For poetry is written out of incompletion, at its peak out of a hunger deeper than the stomach and the body. The simpler incompletion gives us the great voice of man's simpler wills; let these be filled, not to surfeit, and the sensitive man or woman throbs to deeper, higher hungers, at times phrased as a longing for god, or for some reach toward truth, that ungraspable hypothesis of reality behind the ever-dissolving infinitude of illusions. Miss Lowell's pain came from more obvious sources; her poetry is correspondingly obvious. Her pain came from unique and non-general causes; her poetry is unique and correspondingly non-general. Yet she did well all that she could do; and the most that the critic can do is to point out that, after all, the Indian

184

pipe is not a mountain.   But it was never meant
to be a mountain.   Amy Lowell, neither distinguished poet nor great critic, was still Amy
Lowell, and played her part well.   The rest may
ultimately be largely silence.